Values

Andreas Urs Sommer

Values

Why We Need Them Although They Don't Exist

Translated from the German by Paul Richards

palgrave
macmillan

Andreas Urs Sommer
Philosophy
University of Freiburg
Herbolzheim, Baden-Württemberg, Germany

Translated by
Paul Richards
Cornwall, UK

ISBN 978-3-031-42158-7 ISBN 978-3-031-42159-4 (eBook)
https://doi.org/10.1007/978-3-031-42159-4

This Palgrave Macmillan imprint is published by the registered company Springer Nature Switzerland AG.
The registered company address is: Gewerbestrasse 11, 6330 Cham, Switzerland

Paper in this product is recyclable.

Preface

There are some things I think I understand, to an extent at least. I consider the question of such things' existence to be settled. They include stones and stars, pendulums and people, balloons and books.

Some other things I have difficulties understanding. To assume their existence takes effort. These include God and goblins, yetis and unicorns, vampires and values.

True, there are some people who write books about goblins, yetis, unicorns, and vampires, and even more people who talk about God as if He exists. But in a secular, democratic society, no one is required to believe in the presence of goblins, yetis, unicorns, or vampires. Even the societal compulsion to believe in God has evaporated as our culture has moved into modernity. It's up to every individual to do so or to refrain from doing so.

But it's different with values. Is not every last one of us compelled to believe in them—in their existence, their effectiveness, their obligating character? Deny them and you're liable to be thought not just unreliable and selfish but an intellectual terrorist, a nihilist, an enemy of humanity. Is our society not ruled today by an obligation to believe in values? Any values at all—just as long as they're values!

The questions this book asks are thus quite simple: What are these things called values that I'm supposed to believe in? Why should I be compelled to believe in them?

Very simple questions, it would seem. But questions that easily entice us into a many-hued rainforest of uncertainties. The purpose of this book isn't to chop down the jungle. It's to find at least one of many possible paths. "From a statistical perspective, life consists of 98 percent uncertainty. The rest is metabolism."[1]

If you and I are compelled to believe in values, that would seem to presuppose that "values" are not merely words but entities that must somehow exist outside of language. If so, a purely linguistic analysis, that's to say, an investigation into what we say and how we speak when we talk about values, wouldn't be enough to understand what values are and why. But such an analysis could give us some pointers. Useful pointers that might also help to soothe the bad temper that overcomes some when faced with the ever-present values discourse. Anyone, and especially anyone with a voice in politics or the media, who doesn't make stridently clear how they "live by" their values, how important "values-based education" is to them, how much culture depends on values, and how generally indispensable values are, is unfit to be elected or even tolerated. Meanwhile, this values discourse often conceals the concrete interests that are actually inspiring the values-espouser. But this insight, which tempts us to generalize that the term *values* is a mere disguise for interests, is superficial and short-sighted. Clearly, values can, do, and are more than this. But what? What specific benefit is there in discovering or inventing values, prescribing them, or placing yourself under their authority?

These two questions—what values are and why we have them—are joined by a third: What does it say about our society that it needs, of all things, values? What meaning does it have, what purpose does it serve, for a society to define itself via values? In "our" society, there's clearly an insatiable need to talk about values and define ourselves as a community based on shared values. From a historically informed standpoint, this self-confidence in defining what's inherent and relevant to our society through values is somewhat surprising, because it was only really in the nineteenth century that "values" started becoming what they are today. Earlier societies, certainly, had extolled virtue, beauty, and truth, but never "values" as the exclusive and universal benchmark of societal and personal self-understanding. Values are a young phenomenon, one that remains in fashion despite all the upheavals of modernity. The three main questions this book asks thus lie within a single purview, encompassed by one genealogy of morality and of modernity: How did it come to be like this?

Aristotle (384–322 BCE) was conversant with virtue, beauty, and truth, but not, by contrast with us moderns, with anything called "values." He engaged deeply with the question of how we can speak about anything at all. That's why he developed his Categories.[2] His questions are applied here in modified form to "values": What is a value? How many values are there? Of what is a value constituted? To what do values relate? Where and when are values (in use)? In what position is a value? What do values have? What do they do? What is done to values? And, finally, the question asked above, which has no equivalent in Aristotle's categories: Why values?

Nevertheless:

1. This book isn't about human morality (or even: the morality of animal life forms) in general. Every society has an above and below. Often they're called "good" and "evil" or "good" and "bad." But only modernity, only our society, operates with "values" to balance out its above and below, as well as its left and right. That's what the focus is on here.
2. This book laments neither the supposed "collapse of values," nor the "decline of the values-based order," a specter that haunts the opinion pages and letters to the editor, nor the ostensive "values amnesia" that retains a firm place in the discourse in those (sadly ever fewer) establishments where people meet in real life to put the world to rights. This book doesn't attempt some general moral rearmament, nor does it prop up some plea for old or new "value-based" courses of action. Its project is more prosaic, colder. To repeat: It wants to find out what it means and what it says about us, that our society believes it must define itself through values.
3. Ultimately this book doesn't pursue the goal of reviving capital-P Philosophy as a "science of values." When philosophy had attained the peak of its academic self-confidence, one of its guardians, Wilhelm Windelband (1848–1915), could proudly announce that it must be understood "as the science of the necessary and universally valid value judgments. It questions whether there is a science, i.e. a way of thinking, which possesses the value of truth with universal and necessary validity; it asks whether there is a morality, i.e. an intending and an acting, which possesses the value of goodness with general and necessary validity; it asks whether there is art, i.e. a looking and a feeling, which possesses the value of beauty with general and necessary validity."[3] Even for those who most fervently celebrate the cult of values today, the faith in philosophy's ability to

> define and shape values has run dry, especially as philosophy's claim to scientificness is built on shifting ground. Admittedly, this doesn't stop anyone from coolly weighing up the advantages and disadvantages of values for life, and for life in modernity.

Everyone's talking about values. But no one seems to reflect on what it means that everyone's talking about values. Or to think about what values actually are. This book is an attempt to make up for both these omissions. Even if values should turn out to be fictions, they might be useful fictions.

Herbolzheim, Germany Andreas Urs Sommer

Notes

1. Dieter Nuhr : Das Geheimnis des perfekten Tages. Cologne 2015, p. 18.
2. Aristotle: Categories1b 25–27 (Aristotle: Categoriae et Liber de Interpretatione. Recognovit brevique adnotatione critica instruxit L. Minio-Paluello. Oxford 1961, p. 5).
3. Wilhelm Windelband: Präludien. Aufsätze und Reden zur Einleitung in die Philosophie. 3., vermehrte Aufl. Tübingen 1907, p. 45.

Funding

The translation of this work was funded by Geisteswissenschaften International—Translation Funding for Work in the Humanities and Social Sciences from Germany, a joint initiative of the Fritz Thyssen Foundation, the German Federal Foreign Office, the collecting society VG WORT and the Börsenverein des Deutschen Buchhandels (German Publishers & Booksellers Association).

Contents

CHAPTER 1

Existence Is Overrated. What Is a Value?

Abstract This chapter explores the origin and proliferation of values in philosophical discourse. Beginning with the question of why society emphasizes values and their role, the chapter delves into the proposition that values promise quantifiability, variety, and world-structuring power. The narrative traces the historical evolution of values, questioning the notion that philosophy remained detached from values until the nineteenth century. Instead, values discourse originated within economics, intertwining economic and moral perspectives. The chapter scrutinizes how philosophers appropriated and transformed the concept of values, liberating them from economic confines to encompass diverse aspects of human existence. This philosophical transformation allowed for the moralization and globalization of values discourse. The chapter concludes by highlighting the complexity of values' influence, negating the notion of a single dominant value and suggesting a moralistic colonization of human lifeworld through values.

Keywords Values origins • Quantifiability • Variety of values • Philosophical discourse • Economic influence • Hegemony of values • Moralization • Values diversity

A. U. Sommer, *Values*,
https://doi.org/10.1007/978-3-031-42159-4_1

The discrepancy is plain to see: On the one hand, if contemporary discourse is to be believed, the existence of values is a granite-hard certainty. There aren't many things that seem so incontrovertibly to exist as values, if the frequency with which we call on them in daily communication is any indicator. On the other hand, it's clear that no one knows what these things are of whose existence we're so tirelessly certain. At least, if you ask, you'll get at best a shrug of the shoulders and at worst indignation, as if everyone should intuitively be clear about what values are. But I'm not clear, and nor, it seems, is anyone else, when you ask them. It seems, in fact, as if the existence of values is somewhat precarious.

If you investigate *what* values are, you also need to find out *whether* they are and, if so, *in what way*. If values were easily graspable, simple language-products—similar to interjections like "whoops!" and "here, kitty-kitty!", or hesitation sounds like "um" and "hmm"—no one would insist that values are entities existing outside language and the mind, things that are definitely *out there* somewhere, but with a decisive influence on what we *in here* should do and refrain from doing. But this is precisely the insistence with which we're constantly and remorselessly confronted. To inquire into the *what* of values is to try to know what they "really" are, what constitutes them.

Now, no one would deny that people determine the value of phenomena by acting, thinking, and feeling. Living means evaluating—preferring one thing over another. We evaluate situations, opportunities, people, sensations. These evaluations are the expression of preferences; they reflect the perspectives and interests of those doing the evaluating. These evaluations define the evaluators' lives. In an elemental sense, evaluating neither requires a highly organized consciousness nor entails anything specifically human: If I value chocolate ice cream more highly than spinach, this evaluation is based not on any intensive work of reflection but on my gut feeling, one that may run contrary to my "rational" health interests. My family's young tomcat often evaluates the option to romp around the field, hunting all manner of small creatures, as superior to the reality of the bowl that I fill up with food and place in front of his nose. He relates every noise to himself—the rustling of a plastic bag puts him into a state of panic, while the banging of his bowl on the floor evokes optimistic euphoria. Clearly, in his youthful high spirits, he's under constant pressure to evaluate because he relates everything that happens around him to himself. Aging flattens out this evaluatory drive; as he grows, the tomcat will mostly sleep and let his surroundings be. Tomcat wisdom is not dissimilar to human wisdom.

Evaluating means appreciating and assessing that which is and that which could be. Evaluating implies comparing: Even if I evaluate something as entirely negative, I can only do so in comparison with other things—things that I appreciate, that I value highly. The act of evaluating requires neither language nor that quality the self-important members of the species *homo* like to attribute to themselves, namely: "reason." The tomcat can evaluate just as I can—in each case in relation to things that seem relevant to our different lives.

In brief: Evaluating is an activity without which animal (including human) life wouldn't be possible. It structures the reality of the evaluator, arranges it, and categorizes it according to aspects of desirability: For the hungry, consuming food is preferable to forgoing food, and vice versa for the over-nourished. Evaluating requires there to be someone who evaluates—whether this "someone" is an individual human or animal, a group of people, or a whole species.

But do you have to use values to evaluate? That's to say, does it not ineluctably follow from the fact that living beings are evaluating beings that there are values? If your answer to this question is yes, you can drape your thesis in a noble and transcendental-seeming philosophical argument. Always, when we talk about values, when we demand their abolition or their revival, when we bemoan their tyranny or the waning of their influence, we presuppose that there are values. The precondition for the possibility of any evaluating, we say, is values—regardless of whether we utter the actual word "value" or not. Human life is values-based. The discovery of values in the nineteenth century, when philosophy suddenly started talking about them, is one of the great advances of human history: From then on it was possible to endlessly and eagerly explore and investigate the continent of values—a continent that was previously unknown, even though it had always been there.

It's an appealing argument. But as impressive as the expedition reports of the Columbuses of values may sound, and as convincing as the contention of *a priori* presupposed values seems at first glance, there's a problem. The reports are misleading; the argument is false. True, evaluating is a fundamental function of life. But in no way can you derive from this the existence or the "validity" of an abstraction called "value" or of corresponding abstractions in the plural. The idea of value or values as the supposed basis for evaluation is misguided—you could call it, in Wittgenstein's words, a "battle against the bewitchment of our intelligence by means of language."[1] If we spoke of "appraising" instead of "evaluating," we wouldn't assume there was some quality called "praise" just waiting for us to discover. You don't need values to be able to evaluate. It's more the case that evaluating, when it becomes explicit, is itself the act of attributing value and values. But these are *accidental* attributions, not inherent to the thing itself: To evaluate is thus to attribute a particular value, that is, a quality, to a thing or a circumstance. If I evaluate, I don't claim insight into some portentous essence of values, nor any reality or existence of these values independent of the thing I'm evaluating.

"Valuable" is a quality among other qualities—like "red," "in the corner," "hard to make out." The quality "valuable" doesn't participate in some mysterious way in a substance called "value." It's clearly not a quality that belongs to the circumstance, the matter, the thing as such—as physical qualities do, for example—but rather a quality that directly depends on the perspective of the person who attributes it. A glass of water is extraordinarily valuable for a thirsty person in the desert, but thoroughly dispensable for a rain-soaked monsoon victim. The physical and chemical traits of water remain the same. Evaluations are needs-based; the evaluator lends the things their value depending on her circumstances. Values aren't something that precedes evaluation. They emerge from evaluation. Values are not provided but derived. They're not the premise of evaluation but its outcome.

At this point, a card-carrying values ontologist might counter that all this might well apply for values that are within our own power to attribute, but that the true values, the values that ethics as a scientific discipline deals with and that call the shots for morality, are of a completely different nature. They're not the result of an attribution; they precede all attribution. These types of values are the ones that were only discovered in the nineteenth century. The values ontologist doesn't believe, as some do, that there was an unlawful incursion from the economic domain into the moral one, when values suddenly started spreading like an epidemic. The values ontologist's view is that it was only when the economists started talking about values that everyone else's eyes were opened and they became receptive to the true values, the ones that really do stand behind all our evaluations.

The card-carrying values ontologist, therefore, disputes that moral values stand in some direct genetic, let alone causal, relationship to the economic values; he can't get behind the notion of the non-sexual reproduction of economic values into moral values through cell division. There's no magic formula that makes one suddenly into two. For the card-carrying values ontologist, not even parthenogenesis, the virgin birth of moral values, is an option. For him, no explanation in which values become what they are will do because he believes they have always been and will always remain timelessly valid. The values were there; it just took a long time to discover them.

In other words: As the values ontologist sees it, there's a confusion going on between two values concepts or an equivocation between two quite different states of affairs. On the one hand, there are values as the structuring principle of all morality; on the other, by contrast, there are values as subjective attributions to particular objects. In the first case, values are supposed to be substances, things that exist in themselves; in the second, they are mere accidents—something that may be attributed to other things, but may also be de-attributed. For these things themselves, the value that is ascribed to them has no essentially determining relevance.

For the moment, let's let this objection stand. Nonetheless, as someone who has no intuitive values awareness, or at least doesn't know whether or how he has such a thing as values (and would therefore have to be enlightened about his intuitive awareness by an intuitionist expert), I'd like to understand what it means when someone assumes moral value (in contrast to economic value) is a "thing in itself." And what kind of values are these? How can we be constantly discovering new values when, according to the card-carrying values ontologist, values can't come into being but have always eternally been there?

For those of us lacking in values intuition, it does indeed seem as if these "values in themselves" are nothing more than generalized subjective perspectives and preferences: One prisoner, rating freedom more highly than security, proclaims "freedom!" as a universal value, while their cellmate prefers security to freedom and cries "security!" to their own values heaven. And ultimately the sole meaning of these august words is merely that one person wants to get out of the dungeon as quickly as possible while the other is happy to continue enjoying its food and shelter.

So when we non-values-intuitives hear these grandiose words that we're entreated to accept as universal values, we get the feeling we're being sold highly concrete and, by the way, highly divergent wishes, legitimized by being translated into the most generalizing formula possible. The banker understands freedom quite differently from the prisoner; the revolutionary differently from the religious devotee. And yet they all proclaim their devotion to “freedom,” supposedly a value-in-itself, while deriving very different conclusions from it for the ways in which they act and think.

The fact that value judgments depend on perspectives and persons, however, doesn’t have to shake, even for the briefest moment, the card-carrying values ontologist’s faith in the reality of values. After all, it in no way follows from the fact of people’s having quite different views about values, of their prioritizing and naming them differently, that values don’t exist. Clearly, most of the things whose existence is completely undenied are perceived from different points of view by different people. The loaf of bread sitting on the garden table might be a stone to the person who sees it from 100 yards away but, to the person who encounters it first with their nose, it’s a symphony of aromas. If a shadow falls on the loaf, it looks burnt; if a ray of sunlight falls on it, it seems half-baked. It doesn’t follow from the subjectivity of values that they don’t “really” exist—that they’re just the imaginings of the people who proclaim them.

But however the loaf might be subjectively perceived, everyone who knows what bread is will agree that it needs to be baked, that it principally consists of milled grain, and that it serves for human nourishment. To those who eat it, therefore, there’s just as little point pondering the essence of bread as there is its existence. The card-carrying values ontologist will pipe up here and try to resolve any doubts about essence and existence by interposing that man cannot live by bread alone. While bread serves the cause of nutrition, values serve the good of humanity. “Contributing to the good” is what makes a value a value.[2] Since there are things, attitudes, acts, and mindsets that contribute to the good, it’s clearly the case that there are values.

But the concerns are still very much on the table, right next to where the bread was a moment ago. By this reasoning, the loaf of bread, being something that contributes to the good of the people who eat it (as long as they don’t over-indulge), would also be a value, or at least contain value. Let’s put aside for now any quibbles that the definition of values as “contributing to the good” leaves open what “the good” means and whose good it is anyway. “Contributing to the good” seems to be what logicians call a two-part predicate: It’s about the relationship between two objects; something brings about good for another thing. That which increases the good of one person might not be so beneficial to the good of another person, let alone the good of an ant or an albatross. Does the values ontologist have to assume a kind of “über-good” that benefits everyone and everything? And can this “contributing to the good” as a two-part predicate be a thing in itself if it's always only that which it is—good—for other people and other things?

Nit-picking aside, however, I want to take the definition of a value as that which contributes to the good at face value. What precisely does this face value consist of in the business of philosophizing? Firstly, that the definition promises us a crystal-clear criterion for what a value is. Anything that doesn't contribute to the good (or isn't itself the good) is not a value. An obligation, for example, would not be a value if fulfilling it didn't increase the sum of good in the world. Secondly, the definition promises to achieve order in the tangle of values diversity. It would mean there was only one true value remaining—the good—and all other values would have to be measured against it, ranked into more or less successful candidates for valueness. A value called "the good" would be, if not, the actual Platonic ideal of the Good itself, then at least a decent substitute for it. Only to the extent that something participates in this ideal is it good. Only to the extent that a thing participates in the good is it a value.

A yawning sinkhole of questions opens up here, one that I intend to simply sidestep and forget about. Who will care that it's not remotely clear how participating is to be understood, or whether something that contributes to the good does so by increasing it quantitively or calculably, making the good a value in a countable, predictable sense and potentially stopping it from being a transcendental greatness—the precondition for the possibility of value in the first place? The sidestepping and forgetting move certainly makes life easier. But I don't want to forget the fact that the confirmed values ontologist, with his bold über-value of the good and of the contributing-to-the-good, condemns all other values to accidentality, insofar as they are values. If contributing to the good makes something a value, then this is a quality. That which is attributed this quality may well itself be all manner of things—for example, an attitude, an act, or a slice of bread—to which, depending on the circumstances, the questionable quality is then applied. There would then be no values in themselves—aside from the über-value "the good"—except in derived, participatory, accidental form. For the card-carrying values ontologist, that might be a sobering finding.

It's also sobering that, in this structure, the values of morality are no longer differentiated in any way from the values that the economists have been claiming for their own sphere for centuries, in the classic formulation of William Stanley Jevons (1835–1882): "Repeated reflection and inquiry have led me to the somewhat novel opinion, *that value depends entirely upon utility.*"[3] To the hardened moralist, the toppling of the border fence between the domains of morality and market, the reduction of all values to a source called the good or utility, is an outrage. For him, the attempt to rescue the existence and reality of values by demonstrating how they contribute to the good is a Pyrrhic victory, one that will ultimately annihilate all values as entities in their own right and their own essence.

Sadly, however, I can take no such sensibilities into account. That which drives the hardened moralist to fury will comfort the seeker of simplification. If all values flow from one source, the world doesn't fall apart into irreconcilable domains. Morality can now be playfully offset against economics and politics. Let us therefore pause for a rest next to this great promise of the good as the lowest common values denominator. On this isle of tranquility, all secondary values that are derived from the good are attributions, accidents; they're not *a priori* essences but qualities of other things. There's only one value, the good, that the serene islanders have rescued *as a substance*—it's more than a mere figment, they defiantly insist to the shipwrecked mariners who wash up on their shores, although they'll happily admit that all other values are nebulous things, values only by the grace of the one great value-of-values.

The stranded sailor counters that this is a values-realist fallback position taken by islanders unable to demonstrate the real existence and objectivity of ethical values[4] in any way that might function as a precondition for all our valuing. Only marginally less tranquil, our islanders reply that it would be absurd to speak of values and their existence like we talk of building blocks or gummy bears and *their* existence. What really matters is to separate existence and validity. So what is a value? "We need this word, which designates a concept that can no more be defined than the concept of existence, for entities that don't exist but are nevertheless 'something,' and the best way for us to express this is to say they *apply.*"[5] Philosophy no longer has any other duty than to be a "*science of values* [...] but not as the science of the being of values, because a value does not exist, but as the science of the valid, and thus also as the doctrine of the *should* that emerges as soon as valid values are related to a subject that takes a stand on something."[6]

Visibly impressed by this elegant sleight of hand, the stranded mariner can only note that validity is valid only in the manner that money is—as long as no one withdraws the credit. Like existence, she says, validity is infused with the odor of transience. Against this, even the neatest separation of existence from validity achieves little.

From the Isle of Tranquility, the shipwrecked mariner looks longingly out to sea. For insular needs, the cult of a supreme value named the Good and a sacred precinct called Validity may be enough, but for the open seas, probably neither will suffice. Like other animal life-forms, humans are subject to a compulsion to evaluate. They've never relinquished their endless acts of evaluation, but at some point, in contrast to other animal life-forms, they started propagating values as entities upon which they claimed to be basing these acts of evaluation. To the impartial observer, however, it's not so much values that are at work here as biological necessity. Animals, including humans, are choosing beings who are what they are in large part as a function of what they choose. Choosing means evaluating—distinguishing the congenial from the detrimental. "Of course," the tranquil islanders will shout at me, "there it is again, the supreme value, the good!"

It's just a pity that the goods of different life-forms are so often incompatible: The good of the lion is the un-good of the antelope; the good of the rainforest ecosystem is the un-good of the desert ecosystem; the good of my techno-loving neighbor is the un-good of my peace of mind. The sum of all goods doesn't add up to some cosmic total good. My good is choice and decision—and very often some life-form has to pay for it with its un-good: the cow whose steak I eat, as well as the chives with which I garnish the steak. My good-value contradicts the good-values of others. If my natural and cultural equipment requires me to choose what's good for me, what brings me benefit, and by evolutionary extension serves the good of my group and species, then there's nothing particularly noble or honorable about that. It's nothing more than an inescapable biological and cultural mechanism.

To take the fact of evaluating and derive from it values that somehow exist or apply in and of themselves seems, from this perspective, a shameless strategy for retrospectively justifying whatever we would and must do in any case, which is to say: evaluate. Anyone postulating such values is trying to create the impression that a particular choice emerges not from the evaluation function of life itself but from another, incomparably nobler, source. But any proof that there's some kind of causal connection between the postulated values and the acts of evaluation, some kind of genetic relationship, remains to be found. Faced with the moral grandeur of the values preacher, the listener falls into a trance-like state.

Shake off this reverie, however, and you realize that evaluating is nothing more than a compulsion rooted deep in the history of categories, one that some values thinkers like to talk up by hypostasizing values—thus serving their own preferences, their own desire for importance. If it turns out to be a specific feature of human existence to critically distance ourselves from compulsions that our animal nature inflicts on us—and that's what the big word "freedom" was invented for—then maybe it would be feasible to abandon evaluations. That's only possible to a limited extent, because our reality is always a pre-evaluated reality, a reality "tidied up" by our needs and interests, and one that fundamentally differs from the realities of amoebas, ants, and albatrosses.

But humans are beings who can stand back from their own evaluations, from their always pre-evaluated realities. We realize that our world is a world we don't discern neutrally, but one we furnish according to our own needs—in line with our sensory and neurological equipment. Admittedly, this equipment doesn't allow us to suspend our always-pre-evaluated realities by, for example, suddenly gaining direct sensory impressions from the subatomic or superlunary realms—our eyes of their own volition can discern nothing there, because these realms in the first instance play no part in our reality, and our sensory apparatus isn't calibrated for them. But even if, in terms of the practicalities of perception, our boundedness to reality leaves us either helpless or dependent on technical aids (like electron microscopes or telescopes), intellectually we're still able to distance ourselves from the always pre-evaluated realities of our perception and our personal and species-based preferences. Evaluating isn't a particularly upmarket form of human activity. It's not distinct from lesser forms of mere perception, as many values fetishists tend to assume, but is simply the normal state of access to reality for animals, including hominids. Evaluating doesn't stand for an elevated level of reflection but, often, for a lack of it. A philosophy that aspires to reflectiveness will strive to overcome this predilection for values, which in fact is a predilection for evaluating; that's if it can't simply shut the predilection down in the first place. Much as we must, in the daily living of our lives, remain evaluating beings, we do at least have the possibility of partially, experimentally, suspending our evaluating.

If we were to do so, we'd hardly be the first to try removing ourselves philosophically from the ever-present evaluation compulsion. In the early twentieth century there was a vehement clamor for scholars to be "values-free" and critically reflective about the value judgments that resonate in their work as one of the foundations—indeed, one of the values—of scientific methodology.[7] Long before, philosophical practitioners had already tried to remove themselves from the daily pressures to evaluate. One pioneer in this area was Pyrrho of Elis (c. 360–270 BCE), who "introduced and brought validity to the point of view of the incomprehensibility of things and the withholding of judgment"—and not by proclaiming a new doctrine but by leading an exemplary life. "He flinched from nothing and knew no precautions; he showed the same indifference in the face of everything, whether it was approaching wagons or cliffs or dogs or other things of this kind; he allowed the power of sensory perception no influence over himself. But in such cases he owed his salvation [...] to his accompanying pupils."[8] The "withholding of judgment," called *epoché*, characterizes the modes of thought and being of Pyrrho and his imitators. *Epoché* means abstaining from evaluation, suspending all the judgment that we like to make about yes or no, being or not being, commandments and prohibitions. "For nothing is beautiful, nothing ugly, nothing just, nothing unjust; and thus the principle applies without exception to everything that in truth nothing is, but that everything that men do happens for reasons of mere compliance with the law and according to habit; for it applies to every single thing that it is both this and this (other)."[9]

If you take suspension of evaluation as seriously as Pyrrho did, life becomes a difficult and, ultimately, impossible undertaking. You can't evade dogs and obstacles because you refuse to evaluate them; in fact, you might end up walking straight into them if you didn't have disciples by your side with a less rigid approach to your principles than your own. Pyrrho himself was more single-minded: Once, when his teacher Anaxarch of Abdera "fell into a bog, he continued on his way without helping him, a behavior that brought him some disgrace, while Anaxarch himself praised this indifference and detachment in him."[10] But if you practice non-evaluation and non-judgment with unbending consistency, you end up refusing to decide not only what to eat but also whether to eat. If you give up evaluating, you give up deciding—and that's exactly what Pyrrho was striving for. Evaluations, judgments, decisions are detrimental to the peace of the soul. Every evaluation and every decision based on that evaluation could be wrong. You might end up having to regret them. Better, therefore, to do away entirely with evaluating, judging, deciding—or to refrain from them insofar as is possible without sustaining damage to life and limb. The true Pyrrhonist makes himself the plaything of fate and of the evaluations and decisions of others. And he's aware of the fact, indeed, he would celebrate it, if that were not, itself, an evaluation and a judgment.

Pyrrhonism is the expression of a weariness with evaluation in the face of philosophies that think they have to evaluate everything. The philosophers of the Stoa, for example, indulged in an excessive predilection for evaluating; they distinguished things that were valuable because they were in accordance with nature from those that were valueless because they were against nature.[11] For the Pyrrhonist, by contrast, the idea that something could be inherently valuable is an absurdity. That which appears valuable in one respect does not in another respect—a thing is always only valuable for those who consider it valuable. While some modern values realists cling to the chimera that perceiving values is a particularly exclusive and lofty form of perception, the Pyrrhonist holds the tendency of our perception to favor evaluation as responsible for its harmfulness: The evaluation compulsion in all our perception hinders our perception. The value judgments cloud our view of what's there, what's behind or next to the preferences that we bring to bear in our value judgments.

Now, the Pyrrhonists aren't talking about values that, in some mysterious way, are hidden within the problematic practices of accessing—and in doing so evaluating—the external and internal world. The Stoics, their rivals, speak of *axía*, a term that dictionaries translate as "value," "price," "amount," or as "dignity," "service," "wage," or "penalty." But *axía*—or its negative *apaxía*, "unvalue"—is exactly that which is attributed to another thing, the extent to which it is praiseworthy or contemptible. The *axía* of the Stoics isn't something existing in itself; it's something to do with an object.

By contrast, the idea of a substantive existence of values and of their binding force is a rather young, but all the more lushly proliferating, plant in the greenhouse of the mind. For one or two centuries now, the gardeners tending it have been anxious to avoid any contamination of their cultivars with pollen or seeds from outside, since the "value facts are [considered] *primal phenomena*, inaccessible to any further explanation."[12] The outside world is detrimental to the species purity of values and is thus evil—unless the values load it with their goodness and ennoble it. "All values (including the values 'good' and 'evil') are *material qualities* that have a particular order of 'high' and 'low' in relation to each other; and this is independent of the entity in which they find themselves."[13] Faced with these "material values ethics," a heavy dose of skepticism is advisable.

You don't have to follow the Pyrrhonists and view the very idea of evaluating as something pathological that must be banished before a happy life—which means pure drifting—is even possible. To make yourself independent of evaluating is itself to negatively evaluate evaluation—to evaluate it as harmful to the peace of the soul—which thus means that even on this elevated plane you can't avoid evaluation. Regardless, though, if someone wants to hold their evaluating impulses in check and relativize their own evaluation, this seems like a sign of intellectual maturity. To achieve this, you need to at least partially abstain from evaluation (even if not practicing an absolute Pyrrhonic values-neutrality). Evaluating means being involved. Enlightenment means being able to disengage yourself from being involved.

You might perceive that as an achievement or a flaw. Perhaps vacillating between these two sentiments is typical of the age in which we live. In Germany, the generation that came of age at around the time the Berlin Wall fell, dubbed "Generation Golf" in tribute to the car that epitomizes its consumerism, is often accused of having no values. "My brother, the philosopher, asks me about inner values, and I say: yes, those shares still have some hidden potential."[14] Irony turns out to be a powerful weapon for fending off imposed values. "If you think about everything in air quotes, everything is acceptable."[15] So any analysis of the present moment seems to end up having to choose between the unedifying alternatives of values tyranny or values collapse. One side, preoccupied with their individuality and differentness, complain loudly about their feelings of being patronized and see little moral despots everywhere, with nothing better to do than get all up in people's faces on a pretext of "values."[16] The other, primarily concerned with preserving their stability and security, complain even more loudly that morality has lost its connecting power, seeing themselves surrounded by big and little moral wreckers getting all up in people's faces, with nothing better to do than trash people's values. So either we live in a fundamentally over-moralized society, in which only a few libertarian partisans are fighting back against our ultimate silencing through values, or we're in a fundamentally de-moralized society, in which the endless talk of values fails to obscure the fact that all values are *perdu*.

You might be able to do politics with these unlovely alternatives, but you can't do philosophy with them. At least, not if you take one of these contradictory claims for a true diagnosis rather than for what they both really are, which is symptoms. Symptoms that the present thinks it has to define itself through values—even if only *ex negativo*. If you inquire into the substance, the nature of values, you inquire into the substance, the nature of the present, which thinks it has to define itself through values.

But you can't track down the nature of values, and thus the nature of the present, if you only ask the seemingly simple question about the *what* of values and try to strip them down to get to their core—to what really makes them what they are. If you start peeling back the layers, you make the same discovery as when peeling an onion: There's nothing there but more layers.

Values, it's safe to assume, like most other things that people get involved with (themselves included), are historical things—things subject to becoming and dying, like Milky Ways and mayflies. And the idea that even values are historical things—things that it's only recently occurred to anyone to see as the anchor or cornerstone of culture—is a finding that even the most orthodox values realists wouldn't dispute, although they claim we should differentiate between the genesis and the validity of a value, just as we do between discovery and creation. After all, as I've already said, values could have existed for a long time before being discovered. But either way: Even if the values have always been there, if they exist in a human world, they have a history. That's because the human world is, of necessity, a historical world insofar as it's a world in which change is not just appearance but reality.

Friedrich Nietzsche (1844–1900) once noted in parentheses: "Only that which has no history is definable."[17] If you take that not as a dogmatic announcement but as a friendly note on methods, you might feel duty-bound to keep at least some of your focus on the history, the histor*ies*, of values. To place "value" and "values" into historical perspective may mean enquiring into the historicity of the concept and of the word. When did we start to talk about values, to group them together, to collect them under the heading "value," "Wert," "valeur?" A thing denoted by a word or term that has a history or histories might still have existed quite independently before the emergence of the word or term. This will require further probing, because our intrepid venture into the *what* question of "value" has clearly not been exhaustive. Let's continue, therefore, in our attempt to spell it out by following the categories of Aristotle, assuming *pro forma* that values are substances—real somethings. I'll go about this in the "as if" mode—firstly because I clearly didn't manage to get to the bottom of the question about the *what* of the object and, secondly, because I want to state the values realists' case as strongly as possible, that is, to credit values with everything we can get away with crediting them with if they really are substances. I treat values, therefore, as fictive substances that can be declined through all aspects in the category table.

That I personally have difficulties in continuing to believe in a dualism of substance and accidents is by the by. It's more that I assume a more and a less, and understand the world as an interweaving of relationships in which there are things that are more interwoven than others. How interwoven are values? Perhaps they are relationships, not "things?" Perhaps this might also take the sting out of the fight with the values realists, who insist that values are "real." Is it really such an outrageous idea that there are highly divergent forms of reality? Does not the most transient thought, the vaguest feeling, also have a reality? Much of the time, or even most of it, reality seems to imply transience. That applies to humans and gods as well as to thoughts and feelings, visions and values. Even if values are fictions, that doesn't necessarily mean they don't exist.

It may be the case, with regard to phenomena including but not limited to values, that reality is overrated. But even so: "if you have a history, you possess reality."[18]

And another thing that's overrated: existence.

Notes

1. Ludwig Wittgenstein: Philosophical Investigations. In: ibid..:Schriften 1. eds. Gertrude Elizabeth Margaret Anscombe, Georg Henrik von Wright, and Rush Rhees. Frankfurt a. M. 1960, pp. 279–544, here p. 342 (§109).
2. See Peter Schaber: Universale und objektive Werte. In: Martin Endress/ Neil Roughley (eds.): Anthropologie und Moral. Philosophische undsoziologische Perspektiven. Würzburg 2000, pp. 341–357, here p. 350, and Detlef Horster: Das Verhältnis von Normen und Werten. In: Wilfried Härle/Bernhard Vogel (eds.):»Vom Rechte, das mit uns geboren ist«. Aktuelle Probleme des Naturrechts. Hg. im Auftrag der Konrad Adenauer-Stiftung e. V. Freiburg i. Br. u. a. 2007, pp. 202–215, here p. 209.
3. William Stanley Jevons: The Theory of Political Economy. London/New York 1871, p. 2.
4. See John Leslie Mackie: Ethics. Inventing Right and Wrong. London 1990, p. 24.
5. Heinrich Rickert: Der Gegenstand der Erkenntnis. Einführung in die Transzendentalphilosophie. 3. Völlig umgearbeitete und erweiterte Aufl. Tübingen 1915, p. 265.
6. ibid., p. 443.
7. Max Weber: Der Sinn der »Wertfreiheit« der soziologischen und ökonomischen Wissenschaften. In: ibid.: Schriften zur Wissenschaftslehre. ed. Michael Sukale. Stuttgart 1991, pp. 176–236.

8. Diogenes Laertius: De vitis, dogmatibus et apophthegmatibus clarorum philosophorum IX 61 f. (Diogenes Laertius: Leben und Meinungen berühmter Philosophen. Aus dem Griechischen übers. von Otto Apelt, neu hg. von Klaus Reich. Hamburg 1967, Bd. 2, S. 192).
9. Diogenes Laertius: De vitis IX 61 (1967, vol. 2, p. 192).
10. Diogenes Laertius: De vitis IX 63 (1967, vol. 2, p. 193).
11. Johannes Stobaios: Anthologia II 152, 7f (Ioannes Stobaeus: Anthologium, recensuerunt Curtius Wachsmuth et Otto Hense. Libri duo prio res. Vol. II: Librum secundum con tinens. Editio altera. Berlin 1958, p. 83, no. 10 f.).
12. Max Scheler: Der Formalismus in der Ethik und die materiale Wertethik. Neuer Versuch der Grundlegung eines ethischen Personalismus. 4., durchgesehene Aufl. hg. mit einem neuen Sachregister von Maria Scheler. Bern 1954, p. 267.
13. ibid., p. 40.
14. Florian Illies: Generation Golf. Eine Inspektion. 7. Aufl. Frankfurt a. M. 2002, p. 192.
15. ibid., p. 193.
16. See Eberhard Straub: Zur Tyrannei der Werte. Stuttgart 2010.
17. Friedrich Nietzsche: Zur Genealogie der Moral. Eine Streitschrift. In: ibid.: Sämtliche Werke. Kritische Studienausgabe in 15 Einzelbänden. Eds. Giorgio Colli and Mazzino Montinari. 3. Aufl. München/Berlin/New York 1999, vol. 5, pp. 245–412, here p. 317.
18. Friedrich Dürrenmatt: Aus den Papieren eines Wärters. In: Idem.: Gesammelte Werke. vol. 5: Erzählungen. Zürich 1996, pp. 169–213, here p. 171.

CHAPTER 2

Ever More. Where Do Values Come from? And How Many Are There?

Abstract This chapter delves into the complexity of moral values and their role in contemporary society. The author questions the claim that values are becoming increasingly prevalent, prompting the need for control and restriction. The challenge lies in dealing with moral values as units of account, comparable to economic values. The concept of quantifying moral values raises skepticism due to their elusive and shifting nature. Values are seen as both appealing and vague, suggesting precision but often failing to deliver. Despite this, values remain influential, particularly in moral and ethical discussions. The chapter explores how values are invoked and wielded in communication, sometimes explicitly and at other times implicitly. It argues that values, especially moral ones, possess the power to motivate actions beyond self-interest, reshaping priorities. The interplay between moral and economic values is discussed, emphasizing how values diversity emerges as a response to values inflation. The chapter concludes that the dynamic nature of values is integral to the multifaceted modern life, reflecting the evolving complexities of contemporary existence.

Keywords Values inflation • Quantification • Communication • Ethical discourse • Values diversity • Contemporary society • Normative power • Economic values • Values creation

A. U. Sommer, *Values*,
https://doi.org/10.1007/978-3-031-42159-4_2

In our initial peeling of the onion, we had to satisfy ourselves with finding only layers, no core, but the question of the *why* of values can't be ignored any longer. Proceeding from the assumption made at the end of the last chapter, that values are something historical (and perhaps irreducibly so), we are faced with the question of what it is that they promise to achieve that makes a society like ours so ready to speak about them and invoke them? What do values offer that aren't provided by, for example, the virtues, or Beauty, Goodness, and Truth, or the highest principles or our noble duty?

One hypothesis springs to mind: The great promise, the great proposition, of values is, firstly, *quantifiability*. To say "values" is to propose the presence of something precisely definable and measurable, in contrast to the "the good," which is so stark and hard to grasp. With virtues, you have to find a measure, a happy medium, between too much and too little, while values can be set off against each other. With duty, it's only obedience that matters; there's no weighing-up or balancing-out, while values require bookkeeping, and perhaps double- or multiple-entry bookkeeping, with columns for assets and liabilities, amortization and bad debts, silent reserves and reptile funds.

The great promise, the great proposition, of values is, secondly, their *variety*. Values occur in multiples. There's nothing anyone can do to change that, even those who desperately want to establish a monism or monotheism of one value, a monovalorism, in which all values are subsumed under an overarching über-value called the good. The present moment is dominated not by faith in one great value but by values in the plural, or at least by talk of values in the plural. But how many values are there?

The virtues, it's true, have been discussed in the plural for millennia, but from early on they were placed under the diktat of the single overarching virtue that encompasses all the individual sub-virtues. Moreover, the scope of the virtues is limited by the fact of their restriction to the acting, thinking, and feeling of the human individual: They're intended to nudge the individual onto the right path, to mold them. Values, by contrast, are something more than a mere instruction for how to manage ourselves and our lives. According to the claim that has been made for them, they're supposed to give form to the world we live in as a whole.

The great promise, the great proposition, of values is thirdly, therefore, their *world-structuring power*. Those who believe in values tend to believe that values are quantifiable, that there are many of them, and that they significantly determine how we perceive and shape our world—what structure we ascribe to it (and not only the social world but the world as a whole: The values-adherents believe, for example, that values determine even the perception of physical facts, that is, whether these facts are to be assigned relevance and should therefore cross the threshold to conscious perception).

But are these big promises credible? How have values managed to become what this hypothesis claims for them? Let's sketch out the story of how it's been possible for values to become what they seem to be. Some insight into the question of where values come from helps us understand why we can have no definitive answer to the question of how many of them there are.

Putting the *axía* of the Stoics to one side for the moment, for millennia philosophy has been a values-free zone, or at least a zone in which the debates were about goodness, morality, the virtues, but not about "values." It was only in the nineteenth century that "values" suddenly took on philosophical prominence, firstly in the work of Hermann Lotze (1817–1881): "He who talks of that which truly exists is claiming to know that which is in and of itself valuable, not that which is of indifferent value."[1] For the "mind," he argues, a purely causal-mechanical observation of the world doesn't suffice. The mind thirsts for more. The intimation of a higher values sphere, for Lotze, quickly makes itself felt. "In the glorious inner world of youthful fantasies, it comes to awareness that above the usual course of thoughts lies another, essential content which is apprehended as the solely valuable and truly real with all the power of the spirit. This content is ascribed with being neither in itself a single phenomenon nor subject to the limitedness and transience of the finite; as the truly real, that which in all that is phenomenal has being, it cannot be merely an unreal thought of the spirit but possesses the highest quantum of that overarching validity, even outside the thinking spirit, to be that which exists of and for itself."[2]

Trying to put a stop to the indifference that the Pyrrhonists prescribed as a remedy for inner agitation, Lotze here adapts the argument that has been driving philosophers crazy for centuries, the so-called ontological proof of God's existence. The concept of something as perfect as "the solely valuable and truly real" can't have been produced by such an imperfect spirit as that of the "youthful fantasist," and so the thing that this term describes must exist independent of this imperfect spirit, in and of itself. Admittedly, Lotze doesn't credit this new concept of value with so much that he's prepared to completely sacrifice the old terms to it. The top place still goes to the good—it is "the true substance of the world."[3]

At the same time, value had now irrevocably pushed its way into philosophical territory, and its future career would flourish at the expense of the good, which melted into the multiplicity of values. In his polemic against values-thinking as the most decadent effluence of metaphysics, Martin Heidegger (1889–1976) claims: "The values idea, emerging in the nineteenth century as the inner consequence of the modern concept of 'truth,' is the latest and at the same time the weakest offspring of ἀγαθόν."[4] ἀγαθόν, *agathón*, is what Plato (427–348 BCE) calls the good. Heidegger is both right and not right: The genealogical line he draws is correct—the values concept *partly* grew from the good. The sweeping judgment that it's the "weakest offspring" is incorrect. No one could truly believe this values concept, which has unfurled such a rich and broad reception history, to be weak—unless insofar as its broad reception and receivability were to lie precisely in its weakness. But then the weakness would be, well, a strength. Regardless, however, Heidegger was entirely indifferent to all this because he was convinced that philosophy, by moving away from *being*, had been barking up the wrong tree since Plato if not before.

The idea that value is some exclusively moral term, hatched in the incubator of unadulterated philosophical reflection from the larva of *agathón*, had been put into question by critics at a very early stage. The reason was that, in political economy, a discourse about values, which shaped itself into a discourse about values and prices, had long been on the agenda by the time the philosophers first started their tentative approach. Value has its dubious parentage branded on its forehead. It didn't emerge seamless and pure from Plato's ideal; it had co-progenitors who were by no means exclusively interested in the Good, True, and Beautiful.

To a certain kind of philosopher, however, the spread of values discourse into philosophy is a threat. "Colonization," they cry, at what they see not as an independent philosophical innovation but an indicator of imperialism. While the Europeans were seeking to secure their place in the sun on a global scale and in the interests of capital, something else was happening within Europe. An enormous pressure to adapt was building up and, after the collapse of old feudal and ecclesiastical loyalties, it subjected all areas of life, even those that had previously been far removed from the domain of capital, to the logic of economic exploitation. Values, the philosophical freedom-fighter argues, found their way into philosophy as parasites, as creepers that strangle their host trees, and thus was philosophy subjugated to the dictates of economics, which it remains to this day. Values made everything convertible against everything else and forced human beings under the yoke of exploitation, where everything was evaluable. It can therefore hardly be a surprise that philosophers of varying stripes have been caught in the values trap. From neo-idealists like Lotze, neo-Kantians like Wilhelm Windelband or Heinrich Rickert (1863–1936), rogue phenomenologists like Max Scheler (1874–1928), pragmatists like John Dewey (1859–1952), analytical philosophers like George Edward Moore (1873–1958), or aging *enfants terribles* such as Friedrich Nietzsche.

And it's Nietzsche in particular, the philosophical independence fighter, who's treacherous. Firstly, he was the great popularizer of philosophical values discourse and sees man in general and in the first instance as a valuing being: "Man defines himself as the being that measures values, that evaluates and measures, as the 'assessing animal in itself.'"[5] Secondly, this jumped-up philologist preached the complete anti-program to every value that was beloved and dear to the Enlightenment: Instead of equality, he longed for the rule of inequality; instead of democratic decision-making, he wanted the command of the Blond Beast; instead of sympathy for the weak, he urged the ruthlessness of the strong. This Nietzsche is the show pony for an imperialist and capitalist predator morality, in which all that counts is what pays out—in power. And that this particular steed, outfitted with the knightly saddle of the values doctrine as an explicit "transvaluation of all values," should trot into battle to put "the whole world into convulsions,"[6] speaks volumes: Imperialism, capitalism, and values are just different signatures of the infernal machine called exploitation. Philosophy must now, after two centuries of paralysis, shake off the yoke of economics, that values serfdom, in order to smash all values and replace them with principles—principles that are completely incorruptible and can't be bought. Ironically, it was of all people Nietzsche who was the very first to have spoken of *"Christian values,"* albeit with the intent only to denigrate them.[7] The phrase had never occurred to Christians, who were instead preaching "Christian works." "Christian values" only gained currency in the twentieth century, in parallel with the decline of Christian faith. After all, anyone can define "Christian values" in any way they like.

And that's the view from the activist against imperialism and globalization that is the philosophical independence-fighter. There's just one small problem with this memorable picture of an unholy alliance between capitalism, imperialism, moth-eaten Christianity, and values philosophy. It's the fact that values began circulating among philosophers at a time when their economic decline had already begun. This was formulated most incisively during the period leading up to the 1848 revolutions, the *Vormärz*, and shortly after Lotze had hatched his *Metaphysik*, by none other than Friedrich Engels (1820–1895): "The eternal price swings, as created by the competition relation, completely remove the final traces of morality from commerce. There is no more talk of *value;* the same system that seems to place so much weight on value, that lends the abstraction of value in money the honor of a special existence—this very same system destroys through competition all inherent value, transforming the value relation of all things against each other daily and hourly. Where in this maelstrom is the possibility of an exchange resting on an ethical basis? In this continuous to and fro, everyone *must* seek to find the favorable moment for purchase and sale, everyone must become a speculator, i.e., harvest what he has not sown, enrich himself through others' losses, calculate on others' misfortune, or let chance profit for him."[8] It was by no means only among socialist economists that the value of values was in freefall at the moment when the philosophers started helping themselves from the values warehouse. At this point Max Weber (1864–1920) objects that the "failure to coin distinct terms for practical economic- and social-*political* explanations" becomes "outstandingly dangerous." "The chaos wrought by, e.g., use of the term '*value*'—that problem child of our discipline [...], or words like 'productive,' 'from an economic perspective,' etc., which cannot withstand any terminologically clear analysis, is positively unbelievable for the outsider."[9] Economics has long since thrown its "problem child" out with the bathwater—the bathwater it used for the spring cleaning it started in an attempt to become a reliable, ideally mathematical, and rationalized science. The old term, which was somehow supposed to capture a true, inherent value, was neither efficient nor, well, economical, to run.

While Karl Marx (1818–1883), being more philosopher than economist, clung to the romantic idea that the real value of a thing was the labor power and labor time necessary for its production, the objective observer would have to admit that the potential recipients of a product, provided they are free to choose *not* to buy it, are hardly prepared to pay precisely this inner value, as opposed to an approximation of it. It was just as obvious to Marx as it is to us that what actually determines the price of a good is supply and demand rather than labor value, but to him this was a chilling example of the corrupt age of unrestricted rule by capital in which we live. The philosophical freedom fighter may well agree, but he's just as full of mistrust of values as the modern economists who love nothing better than to relinquish values. Moreover, the freedom fighter no longer believes in Marx's ideal labor-time values, instead seeing any talk by philosophers of values as decisive proof that they've placed themselves in the service of the hegemony over our discourse held by economics. What a shame, then, that the economists no longer want to talk about values, just because they've proven that values only *seem* to exist, or that their existence is of secondary importance, or that they don't exist at all.

The fact that the philosophers only took values under their wings when the values habitat in economics was acutely endangered could lead us to conclude that philosophy is an eternal latecomer, Hegel's owl of Minerva fluttering from bough to bough only as dusk falls, with nothing to show for its hindsight. But you can hardly deny that the philosophers have ensured an unprecedented late boom in values—freeing them from their economic big cats' enclosure so that today even the lowliest local politician can't manage to justify a new freeway or excuse a corruption scandal without invoking "values." The philosophers have dissolved the boundaries of values. They've opened up all domains of human existence to the values; they've comprehensively globalized them. The invasion thesis of the philosophical independence-fighter misses the fact that the values haven't simply economized philosophy, and that today's ubiquitous values discourse isn't simply the expression of an economization of our lifeworld.

There's an alternative description that may get closer to the facts of the case. The philosophers sneakily trapped an economic concept, gutted it, stuffed it with new content and pushed it into the arena of cultural-hegemonic conflict, and they did so in order to ensure optimum conditions for the survival of their own interest, that is, the assertion of secular ethics. This explanation relies on the assumption that in the nineteenth century it was indeed the philosophers who generalized and substantialized values, that values weren't just the echo of a contemporary extra-philosophical trend (and if you wanted to play it safe here, you'd have to analyze values discourse in all written sources from this century, not just quantitatively but also qualitatively). In these battles for hegemony, there could be no long-term coexistence with moral law and pure duty in the manner of Kant. By contrast, such archetypal figures as the prudent housewife and the risk-taking speculator were choosing values at a time when no philosopher had ever uttered the V-word. For non-philosophers, this must have made it all the more gratifying when the philosophers started playing their new language game in which "values" no longer just meant the touchstones of bourgeois economic life and now included so much more that was dear to the hearts of the housewife and the speculator: the wellbeing of children, for example, or the honor of the family or the glory of the fatherland. The philosophers were clever enough to talk not just of the one, supreme value, but of values in the plural. It's not an economization that the globalization of the values discourse indicates, then, but a moralization: The rise to dominance of moral modes of thought by means of the categorization of human existence into values, which have thus been recoined from economic to moral terms. So it won't do to simply claim a general "tyranny of values," to borrow a watchword from valorophile fundamental ontologist Nicolai Hartmann (1882–1950),[10] one taken up by valorophobe legal scholar Carl Schmitt (1888–1985) and elevated to a general accusation aimed at the West Germany of his day.[11] To prove tyranny, there would need to be *one* authority, *one* value that had arrogated power over acting, thinking, and feeling. The point of the now-ubiquitous values discourse, however, is that it assumes an unquantified diversity of values that either peacefully coexist or violently compete with each other. If you don't accept a single overarching über-value, one value relativizes the other. That rules out tyranny (although not the possibility that someone might be tyrannized by one specific value). Would it not, therefore, be more accurate to speak of a moralistic colonization of the lifeworld through values?

Philosophy's concept of values, therefore, is more than a mere "latecomer" to moral "goodness" but rather a thing of thoroughly impure origins. It appears like a hybrid lifeform emerging from both morality and economics—and its main source of strength, its ability to find connections everywhere, is the accumulated hereditary substance from two different domains.

But "value" is by no means the first term that has found its way from economics into morality. "Have these previous genealogists of morality even dreamily sensed from afar that, for example, that key moral term *Schuld* ["guilt"] has its origins in the very material term *Schulden* ["debts"]?[12] Debt as a basic concept for the kind of moral reflection, tangible as far back as the oldest testimony of Greek philosophy, the fragment by Anaximander (around 610–547 BCE),[13] assumes that humans are beings that can incur debt—beings that enter into obligations with others to discharge a certain duty in the future. Being able to incur debt and become indebted is based on an evolutionary history that separates the hominids from other animals. So the same thing that has happened, only recently in world-historical perspective, to values—that philosophy has helped itself to a particular concept from economics and broadened it into a universal concept—happened millennia ago to debt. In the beginning, debts were concrete obligations that the debtor had to fulfill to the creditor, but early religion quickly seized onto the idea of an obligation to God, an obligation that seemed impossibly high, so that man, the "sinner," was left in a state of chronic indebtedness.[14] Morality refracted through philosophy—having abandoned the gods—directed that debt inwards. Now we could become indebted not only to other people to whom we owed repayments but also, and in fact above all, to the good, to what we are commanded to do—and, later, to duty. The philosophers took from the priests the task of cultivating guilty consciences.

So there's nothing new about philosophy being in the business of appropriating and expanding particular terms. In fact, it may be that *all* of the incisive philosophical terms are particular concepts that have been globalized, for example from economics, religion, or politics. And if it's now values, of all things, that the philosophers have taken a shine to, that they want to domesticate and release into the wilds of societal life, then this is a long overdue act of penance for having condemned humankind to a life of moral indebtedness for millennia: Values are positive; they compensate for the tyranny of guilt/debt and the compulsion to atone. Values are the expression of a perception of reality made positive, in which everything no longer revolves around guilt, debt, and atonement but also encompasses having and owning.

The philosophers only came upon values (in their unspecified multiplicity) at the moment when the dominant morality was no longer self-evidently moral, when the ideological and religious conditions of what was commanded and forbidden in Old Europe were falling away—specifically, in the eighteenth and nineteenth centuries. Under the pressure of modernization, morality seemed to need a justification—one that, for example, the hedonistic atheists hoped to find in personal wellbeing, the Kantians in reason and reasonably self-imposed duty, and the Utilitarians in the happiness of the greatest number. But these proposals weren't compatible with each other, and some of them couldn't stand up to the scientific developments of the times. The moment when a disenchanted philosophy of history, and with it Darwinism, showed the irrefutable historicity and thus contingency even of human reason *should* have spelled an end to the self-assurance of those who believed in reason as an absolute (admittedly, some still cling to this absolute, unreceptive to any insight into historical contingency, to the relativity of their own perspective, and thus to the reason they hold so dear—as if that reason wasn't the result of human evolution but some unmediated essence).

Values, by contrast, seemed not only to solve the justification problem of non-religious morality—if morality administers values, then it must be valuable itself—but also to bring the various and essentially incompatible philosophical moral theories to a lowest common denominator. The hedonists could pledge allegiance to values just as ardently as the idealists, the Kantians just as much as the Utilitarians—not to mention the Christians and their "Christian values." In their vagueness, values are something that "just works" for all of them. And not just for "professional" philosophers but also, and in particular, for the average, increasingly self-confident, more or less obstreperous citizen in need of a safeguard, or in cases of higher demand for reflection even a justification for their morality, including in business, society, and at home, to secure their morality's validity, its authority. The safeguarding and justification offered by religion were at best rundown, or at least no longer capable of generalization. The citizen could no longer rely on God. So, like the philosophers, she needed a new set of things that could be taken for granted—and noticed that everything that mattered to her were "values." Why should it be any different in morality from how it was in the home, in business, and in society?

At this point, a cultural critic might intervene that this bourgeois weakness for values shows just how unsuitable and, indeed, un-moral they are. Clearly, she reasons, the logic of thinking, feeling, and acting in values is determined by the paradigm of *having*, but, if the choice we face, as Erich Fromm (1900–1980) argued, is between "having and being," the right choice must surely be *being*.[15] At this point I could say in my defense that I am acting here merely as a historian of morality, one who is simply analyzing the emergence and impact of values-thinking. The observation that values-thinking attained a certain attractiveness in a bourgeois context would therefore not be associated with any value judgment, let alone stand as an apology for bourgeois morality. In objection to the allocation of values to the *having* paradigm rather than the *being* paradigm, I could also point out that, remarkably, it is in the vocabulary and self-understanding of those people who claim to orient themselves not around *having* but around *being* that values have achieved a central place. Among environmentalists and human rights activists, religious believers and left-wing activists, recourse to values is an indispensable entry ticket, which means that, empirically, there's absolutely no case for a notable *having* interest among values-believers. But in any case I don't want to expand on these two defense strategies against the cultural critic's argument because I see the whole being/having dichotomy as fundamentally misguided to begin with, the simplistic expression of a radical-chic ideology for SUV-drivers and second home-owners disguised as ideological criticism. You can't have being without having, and having can't exist without being.[16]

What we really should be thinking about, beyond the false alternative between being and having, is the fact that values from the very beginning appear in multiples. The implications of this are more than just that there are various different values. It's also hard to avoid the supposition that there are values that contradict each other and that, despite all our efforts, can't be reconciled to each other. One piece of observable evidence is that many people revere the value of equality, while others revere the value of inequality. The egalitarian may well denounce inequality as a non-value, but the anti-egalitarian will say the same about equality; and there's no means in sight for reconciling this fundamental disagreement on a higher values level—unless some über-value that both sides could recognize, for example the good, came upon the scene. But even if the two warring parties—egalitarians and anti-egalitarians—could nominally agree on an über-value of this kind—after all, who prefers the not-good to the good?—they'll stick to completely contradictory definitions of the good. For one side, the good is ensured when we regard people as fundamentally equal and treat them equally, while for the other side it's only ensured if we regard people as fundamentally unequal and treat them unequally.

If, sooner or later, we have to come to terms with the multiplicity of values, then we also have to accept that any appeal to "values" in such abstraction explains nothing and gets us nowhere. Values as such don't seem to be valuable in themselves—they're always concrete values in concrete structures and concrete relationships. Even our most hated antagonists or political ideologies invoke values, and no one—having once accepted "values" as a viable concept—will be able to deny that values are in play even here. It's just that these aren't the values that we share.

The multiplicity of values pays out in domain transgressions and domain de-borderings. In the pre-modern era, when people hadn't yet started to operate with values in a free-hand and wide-scale way, there was a fenced-off domain of the purely moral: Virtue and sin, good and evil were its guiding distinctions. The modern age is dominated—and characterized—by the blending of domains. Values are the instrument for putting these domains, understood as being in principle separate, into relationship with each other. What were hitherto the guiding distinctions between the various domains have now ceased to be final measures of reference. Values break through the internal order of the intra-domain distinctions and shine them onto a larger, empty projection screen. Values make the domains mutually compatible—especially when they're differentiated. Thinking, feeling, and acting in values makes everything become offsetable against everything else, from the demands of morality or economy to politics or self-actualization, religion or even science. That there must be continuous conflicts because of the way the concrete values emerge from diverse circumstances, priorities, and experiences, will surprise no one. Max Weber found mythological words for these values conflicts: "The many gods of antiquity, disenchanted and thus appearing in the form of impersonal forces, rise from their graves, strive for command over our lives, and resume their eternal struggle among themselves."[17] For all its dramatic rhetoric, however, this insight misses the essential: The fight going on here isn't some eternal battle—and these aren't old gods returning from their crypts. What's happening in modernity under the banner of values is in fact something completely new. In the modern age, values are becoming expansionist and *polemogenous*—they generate argument—because they no longer remain shut up in their separate domains, such as morality, economics, or politics, but are spreading out everywhere. This de-bordering through values exponentially increases the risk of conflict. These values are not ancient gods but very new demons, whose power lies in transgression, not in some drive to subsume everything within morality or economics. Values are aggressive not because they're moral or economic but because they're no longer subject to any domain of life; instead, they break through domain borders.

My story of how values have managed to become what they are runs counter, therefore, to the story told by the philosophical independence-fighter, as well as to the story told by the card-carrying values-ontologist. In this story, values aren't things that exist in and of themselves and are simply waiting to be revealed. But nor are they the villains in a story of naked colonialism, an epidemic of economic thought patterns penetrating the realm of ethics. What's actually happening in the concept of values is the nuclear fusion of the moral with the economic, and that's what determines the plot of this story—a nuclear fusion that led to "values" getting a nucleus in the first place. In the pre-modern world, value was something attributed to a service or a product—like the *valeur* of a painting, its color tones, and gradations. Before the moral-economic nuclear fusion, values were merely the accidents of a substance. In the nineteenth century they became substances themselves, but only *substances as if:* We've started to talk about values as if they were substances. But just talking about them as such doesn't make them that.

In this values origin story, which takes on the form of a salvation story, values achieve substance through the moral-economic nuclear fusion and, at the same time, through their scope; through the claim for validity they gain universality, contour, and materiality. They seem to win their independence from the act of assessing, of evaluating—becoming seemingly untouchable things in themselves. "True values have an independent existence. Otherwise, they would not be true values," wrote the philosopher Kurt Leese (1887–1965) 1935 to the theologist Fritz Buri (1907–1995) in 1935.[18]

This "as if" substantiality of values could be understood as modernity's last metaphysical crutch, one it has held on to after painfully relinquishing the unmediated moral good and the religious sacred. Admittedly, even this "as if" substantiality seems to be a fragile thing. Values don't remain what they are—they're not unshakable rockfaces on the mountain of life. They're extremely dynamic. They seem to multiply. Values bring forth values, and they seem to enjoy the act of reproduction.

How should we approach the problem of values inflation? On a purely diagnostic level? Or therapeutically? And if it has occurred to you that values are never values alone but are always interattached—in context with other values and as integrated into a world—you'll probably ask what it means when values multiply. How does that alter the network of connections?

And the answer to the question in the title of this chapter? How many values? A lot. And ever more.

Notes

1. Hermann Lotze: Metaphysik. Leipzig 1841, p. 13.
2. ibid., p. 6.
3. ibid., p. 326.
4. Martin Heidegger: Wegmarken. In: idem.: Gesamtausgabe. I. Abteilung:Veröffentliche Schriften 1914–1970. Frankfurt a. M. 1976, vol. 9, p. 227.
5. Friedrich Nietzsche: Zur Genealogie der Moral. Eine Streitschrift. In: Idem.: Gesammelte Werke. Kritische Studienausgabe in 15 Einzelbänden.

Hg. von Giorgio Colli und Mazzino Montinari. 3. Aufl. München/Berlin/New York 1999, vol. 5, pp. 245–412, here p. 306.
6. Friedrich Nietzsche: Sämtliche Briefe. Kritische Studienausgabe in 8 Bänden. eds. Giorgio Colli and Mazzino Montinari. 2. Aufl. München/Berlin/New York 2003, vol. 8, p. 482.
7. Friedrich Nietzsche: Der Antichrist. Fluch auf das Christenthum. In: idem.: Sämtliche Werke. KritischeStudienausgabe in 15 Einzelbänden. eds. Giorgio Colli and Mazzino Montinari. 3. Aufl. München/Berlin/New York 1999, vol. 6, pp. 165–254, here p. 250.
8. Friedrich Engels: Umrisse zu einer Kritik der Nationalökonomie. In:Deutsch-Französische Jahrbücher. eds. Arnold Ruge and Karl Marx. Paris 1844, pp. 86–114, here p. 104.
9. Max Weber: Gesammelte Aufsätze zur Wissenschaftslehre. ed. Von Johannes Winckelmann. 6. Aufl. Tübingen 1985, p. 208 f.
10. Nicolai Hartmann: Ethik. Berlin 1962, p. 574.
11. Carl Schmitt: Die Tyrannei der Werte. In: Eberhard Jüngel/Sepp Schelz/Carl Schmitt: Die Tyrannei der Werte. Hamburg 1979, pp. 11–43.
12. Nietzsche: Zur Genealogie der Moral, p. 297.
13. Das Fragment des Anaximander lautet: »Woraus aber für das Seiende das Werden ist, dahinein erfolgt auch sein Vergehen nach der Schuldigkeit; denn sie schaffen einander Buße und zahlen Strafe für ihre Ungerechtigkeit nach der Ordnung der Zeit« (Hermann Diels/Walther Kranz [Hg.]: Die Fragmente der Vorsokratiker. 5. Aufl. Berlin 1951, Fragment 12 B 1).
14. Christianity has elevated this idea to a central doctrine, classically formulated in Anselm of Canterbury's Cur deus homo? (c. 1094–1098): The debt of man is so unendingly great that only a god can pay it. But since man is the debtor, God must become man in order to make recompense.
15. Erich Fromm: Haben oder Sein. Die seelischen Grundlagen einer neuen Gesellschaft. Stuttgart 1976.
16. Andreas Urs Sommer/Dagmar Winter/Miguel Skirl: Die Hortung. Eine Philosophie des Sammelns. Düsseldorf 2000.
17. Weber: Gesammelte Aufsätze zur Wissenschaftslehre, p. 605.
18. Albert Schweitzer/Fritz Buri:Existenzphilosophie und Christentum. Briefe 1935–1964. Introduced, annotated and ed. by Andreas Urs Sommer. Munich 2000, p. 79.

CHAPTER 3

Allure of the Temporary. How Is a Value?

Abstract The allure of temporary values is explored in Chap. 3, building upon the concept introduced earlier. The chapter delves into the intricate relationship between values, their quantifiability, and their potential for universal applicability. Despite the challenges of precisely quantifying or categorizing values, they retain a powerful influence on human behavior and decision-making. The chapter contends that values, particularly moral values, possess a unique ability to motivate and justify actions, often reshaping priorities and perspectives. This interplay between moral and economic values leads to a proliferation of new values as a response to differing moral standpoints. The chapter also investigates how values are invoked in everyday communication, examining their role in shaping individual choices and collective identities. Overall, the chapter highlights the complex dynamics of values, their mutable nature, and their impact on human interactions and societal structures.

Keywords Values • Quantifiability • Moral values • Universal applicability • Motivation • Justification • Values inflation • Everyday communication • Collective identity

A. U. Sommer, *Values*,
https://doi.org/10.1007/978-3-031-42159-4_3

Ever more values? That's what I claimed at the end of the last chapter. Is it true? And if it is true, isn't that an urgent reason to impose control, restriction, values scarcity? Certainly, even morality must obey the modern paradigm of mathematizability, if it believes itself to be determined by values (or if the moral philosophers believe it is). But here's the problem: How can we deal with moral values as a unit of account—the way money as a unit of account enables us to deal with economic values? How, for example, do you offset liberty against equality or fraternity? A quantum of liberty against two quanta of equality and half a quantum of fraternity, garnished with a quantum of solace? The suspicion quickly arises that the problem of the exchangeability of moral values is insoluble. It follows from this suspicion that the presumed exchangeability of moral values, and indeed of all values that can't be added up in numbers or sums of cash, results in nothing more than a superficial pretense of precision. The promise of quantifiability and the promise of multiplicity easily fall into disrepute, and you might be on the point of giving up on the whole values idea before even glimpsing their third promise, that is, their world-structuring power. But it would in any case be premature to dismiss the first two promises because, in practice, the values boom has in no way suffered from the inability of values to be either precisely quantified or comprehensively listed in their great diversity. One significant appeal of non-mathematical values and of recourse to them lies, clearly, precisely in this vagueness. The *word* "values" creates a suggestion of precision that the obscure *thing* "values" doesn't quite live up to. But it compensates—or over-compensates—for this with the prospect of universal applicability. Values are quicksilver, constantly shape-shifting, constantly amalgamable with hard metals, and also toxic. The promise of mutability and ubiquitous applicability makes up for the failure of the promise of quantifiability, while the promise of multiplicity can be grasped above all as a promise of multiplication: The values heap grows—and we seem to feel totally okay about that.

Nonetheless, you'd be wrong to imagine the agglomeration of values either as a fixed structure or as a peaceful coexistence. High-grade instability and high-grade conflict-productivity seem to be inevitable. How, for example, can you harmonize the value of equality with that of friendship? If I devote myself to friendship, I reject the call to treat all people equally and privilege those with whom I want to be friends.

But who actually refers to "values" in their everyday communication—and if so, under what circumstances? When we meet up with friends, we don't tend to proclaim the value of friendship. When we go swimming, we don't usually reflect on the value of health. When we hail a cab, our minds aren't fervently occupied with the value of mobility. And yet all these acts are choices that imply evaluation. We favor an activity that at that moment we rate more highly than another—we meet friends instead of business partners, go swimming instead of hiking, ride a taxi rather than the tram. In all these cases we're evaluating, without recourse to values as as-if substances, without thinking about values at all. Most acts of evaluation get by without explicit values, however much the card-carrying values ontologist, reconstructing these acts after the fact, might see such values as their basis. This projection, this assumption of values, is completely surplus to our requirements at this point. Sometimes, however, and not as rarely as you might think, we really do start dealing in values, explicitly in their as-if substantiality, in our everyday communication. And not just in the kind of utterings in talk shows and election speeches that most of us are never called upon to make. It often happens in situations in which we deviate from expected behavioral patterns to optimize our own wellbeing. It may be that values are much more often invoked in talk shows and elections than under normal circumstances. We could speculate about why that might be the case. The obvious answer is that in talk shows and election speeches you have to visibly celebrate your supra-individual, universally orientated message for everyone ("No, I could care less about gaining power for myself, what matters to me is family values"), as does the pastor in church, who would be lost without values discourse. There are clearly situations—like public speaking—in which to invoke values is to exert a special, positively magical appeal. These special situations generally seem to be ones in which there's no action; just speaking. That is, no one demands in these situations that the speaker turns their words into deeds there and then. The deeds are supposed to come, if at all, later, and if not, you're free to kick the politician back out into the cold, while the pastor isn't expected to do anything other than generate words anyway.

The everyday *action situations* in which values play a role as as-if substances seem to need values above all as a moral power. Perhaps we speak occasionally of a film's "production values," or the "sentimental value" that our grandfather's watch has for us. But in communication, it's the moral dimension, or perhaps the morality-producing dimension of values, that seems to take center-stage. If you appeal to "moral values," you devalue all other possible values that you could bring to bear on an action. Economic or political values—the maximization of income or power—are literally put into the wrong by moral values. Suppose, given the choice of drinking a fair-trade coffee or a regular, "unfairly" produced coffee, I justify my decision to do the latter with aesthetic values (it tastes better) or economic ones (it's cheaper); these values immediately lose their teeth if someone tells me the moral values of justice and of equality require consumption of fair-trade products. In most everyday situations I'll never specifically go into economic or aesthetic values, but I might now and then make use of moral values. These moral values may serve one of two purposes: either retroactively justifying an act that secretly had quite different reasons and causes, or, and this is the claim connected communicatively with any recourse to moral values, these values do indeed have normative and motivating power for our actions. These as-if substances do seem to be capable of pushing our actions in a direction that of themselves, in their autonomy, with their orientation towards such goals as maximum sensual enjoyment or maximum financial profit, they would not have taken. If moral values come into play in everyday action situations, they rearrange the generally accepted mechanisms of striving and being striven for according to individual optimization; they redistribute the weightings. Under pressure from them, I might indeed buy fair-trade coffee, even though it's more expensive and tastes worse. Morality majoritizes everything.

You might be asking how we're defining the "moral" in "moral values" here. For household use I'd recommend using "moral" for those values that claim the authority to guide actions in such a way that they benefit other people (other lifeforms, the wider community, the world), regardless of what connects the actor with the beneficiaries of their actions. That would make a moral value one that either contradicts the self-interest of the actor or is indifferent to it. In contrast to Aristotle's discussion of friendship within the field we have since called "ethics," my proposed household definition does not place friendship within the field of "moral values," because my relationship to my friends is determined by my personal interests, the result of my favoring them over other people. Moral values suggest, at the same time, altruism and charitableness—and that makes them (seemingly) superior to other arguments in the structure of communication, because they move beyond the individual perspectives of the actor to a general perspective.

Values then come to bear—in a motivating or justifying function—in everyday action situations and are (made) visible if, without them, we would act differently, more self-interestedly. And these values, with their ability to reverse polarity, seem to be in the first instance moral in nature.

But let's return now to the alleged nuclear fusion of the moral and the economic that seemed to be characteristic of "values." How do things stand with that? And what's the deal with the multiplication of values?

On the first question: It's clearly the case that values, which tend towards the moral, and which are based on an interior distinction between good and evil or good and bad, retain their atom-melding power. As values, despite the aforementioned difficulties, they retain the appearance of quantifiability, of precision. They have an appellative power different from that of, for example, the good or the virtues. In contrast to the good, which remains in the undetermined realm of universal abstraction, they suggest concretion. And in contrast to the virtues, which are, after all, character traits of the subject, they suggest much greater objectivity. Virtues can't be separated from the person to whom they are attributed; they're the person's accidents or attributes, as distinct from the as-if substantiality of values. The values hold a middle ground between the highly abstract good and the subjectively personal virtues; they lie within the frequency range of human perception, or at least that's what the people who call on them believe. Values evoke the appearance of obligation. They don't actually force compliance, but they imply it.

Which leads us to the second question: How is it that values multiply, that new values emerge? The answer seems obvious: There's no remedy for values except other values. And there's certainly no remedy for moral values except other moral values. If you're confronted with values in everyday communication, you can't appeal to economic benefit or political calculation without putting yourself seriously on the defensive. So you parry with values: Morality requires counter-morality. To counter the values of theism, the values of religious freedom were invented, presenting the religious zealots of the early modern era with something they'd never previously heard of. To counter the values of a civilizing mission for all humanity, the values of self-determination for all peoples were invented, confronting the historical philosophers and colonizers of the nineteenth century with something they'd hitherto refused to contemplate. To counter the values of social hierarchy according to personal merits, the values of social inclusion were invented, a thing our grandparents had never heard of. To counter the values of marriage and the family, the values of free sexual orientation and gender mainstreaming were invented, something we hadn't heard of until recently. The pressure to join in the values discourses leads to values inflation.

Values diversity and values multiplication result from the communicative compulsion to answer morality with morality, which in turn is due to the acute weakness of other argumentation strategies. Some people, those whose highest values include unity, indivisibility, and consistency, are horrified by the idea of values inflation, because they can't reconcile morality and diversity. How can you look on the growing heap of values with its squalling contradictions and still feel at ease?

Perhaps you can feel at ease precisely because the values heap always facilitates shifts of values, the privileging of a new value when an old one doesn't suit you. As soon as moral argumentation patterns take the upper hand in communication situations oriented around dissent rather than consensus, values inflation is inevitable. As soon as everyone feels at home under the roof of a value, the invocation of this value serves only to bolster the collective self; it creates an *us*-feeling and wants to integrate rather than to isolate. If, by contrast, the value is used to uphold a position in the face of resistance, the other side only has two routes available to it if it doesn't want to get into fruitless debates about value. The first route is to respond to the weighty value that the antagonist has fed into the dispute by accepting it, by getting under the same values roof as the antagonist, while simultaneously claiming that the antagonist is interpreting the value wrongly and deriving the wrong conclusions from it ("You talk about the Christian value of compassion, to which I also commit myself, but you wrongly conclude that Muslim asylum-seekers shouldn't be included in this compassion, because they're not Christians"). The second route involves establishing a counter-value that you claim is at least equal to or ideally greater in importance than the antagonist's value ("You talk about the Christian value of compassion, but the real value is unconditional love for all living beings, a value that has freed itself from any religious associations," or alternatively, "You talk about the Christian value of compassion, but we should really base our actions not on compassion but on reason").

In order for there to be a free debate—that is, a debate in which participants from different ethical traditions can reach compatible conclusions—about how we should live *in abstracto* and *in concreto*, we need the option of moral values creation. A single glance at the myriad pieces of communication in which values are drawn on is enough to show that much use is made of this option, especially because values, despite the suggestion of offsettability inherent to the very concept, often cannot in fact be offset against each other. In practice, values are often created through evasions, that's to say, through the moral colonization of a space that was previously not morally colonized (or not in the same way). It would have been just as impossible to convey to a Roman emperor the idea that a people was something whose self-determination was a moral value as it would be to convey to a pope the idea that free sexual orientation is a moral value. So moral values-creation fences off tracts of virgin territory and plows them over in an attempt to deter values-incursions from other plots. These it denounces as illegitimate on the grounds that they're not applicable to the particular case and location under dispute. If you keep on digging into the *how* of values—and after all that's the question posed at the start of this chapter—it seems natural to observe that the fact of moral values-creation is systematically obscured in those communication and action situations in which values are brought to bear.

If you keep on digging into the *how* of values—and after all that's the question posed at the start of this chapter—it seems natural to observe that the fact of moral values-creation is systematically obscured in those communication and action situations in which values are brought to bear. Reclaimed values must not appear in these situations, it seems, as something emerged, contingent, and thus made. The comforting fiction of these communication and action situations has its basis in designating values as legitimizing foundations for actions. To this end, these values must be passed off as already existing in and of themselves. The communicative existence of values draws significant strength from avoiding precisely the impression that the sober observer will hardly be able to avoid: The impression, that is, that values only emerge when created communicatively or reflexively. No one takes offense at the claim that *virtues* emerge only when produced—when we act them out—but *values* are supposed to defy all contingency, to be as-if substances. There's no more energetic objection to this than that of the historian, who notes that history has repeatedly demonstrated that values are subject to change or at least that the weightings of values are subject to change—and moreover that values exist only after being called into life by rhetoric. But that doesn't trouble the moral pawnbroker, enthusiastically weighing values up on his scales, in the slightest.

The card-carrying values ontologist will object to the values inflation hypothesis on the grounds that it's not the values that are multiplying but the glib talk of values. Not values inflation, therefore, but merely values-talk inflation. Essentially, he argues, we just have more names for the same things, because the fundamental values, the values at the highest level, remain the same. The obvious response to the values ontologist is to ask him to be so good as to say what these unchanging and non-inflatable fundamental values are—freedom, for example, has held very different states of relevance and irrelevance over the centuries, so seems an unlikely candidate. Perhaps we have so many more values today because we own more things, because we carve out our existence in many more and different areas. The pluralization of our lives requires the pluralization of values. We need different values for all the different areas of our lives, because these lives, in contrast to lives in traditional societies, have highly varied facets. This polymorphism of our modern life can't be hammered into shape on the simple anvil that sufficed for the good; it can't be surveyed with a single set of supposedly fixed weights and measures.

It's in this proliferation of new life circumstances that the deeper reason for values inflation lies. It's not just that the conditions of human existence have changed (they do that constantly), it's that they've also proliferated; and for every single one of these conditions we need to tweak and modify the values repertoire. In Western democratic societies we are seeing not just the phenomenon that sociologists discuss under the heading "value change," that is, a shift in the focus of collective preferences and individual orientations, but also, and more importantly, the broadening of this focus as a result of proliferated circumstances. At the same time, the values repertoire is being very frequently and very elegantly tweaked and modified through the invention of new values that make it vastly easier to find one's way in different circumstances. Different milieus cultivate different values, but we've gotten used to being members of diverse milieus ourselves. When values shift or proliferate, the old values don't—or don't necessarily—die off. A young Muslim man who upholds the values of the interest-charging economy at work and the values of relaxed hedonism with his non-Muslim friends might remain loyal to the ancient value of honor in his relationship with his sister—and with her relationship to these values. The conflict of values in one person seems to be experienced as less debilitating than the looming threat of values-emptiness, of a potential values-abstinence under new circumstances. How should the young Muslim behave if his non-Muslim friends invite him to a party? Is not the simplest thing to slip into a new values outfit for a few hours?

New values often seem to perform more effectively in a new situation than the established value set. Two examples: Mindfulness, which is absent from the classic Western virtues catalogs and has its roots in an occidentalized neo-Buddhism, is currently enjoying something of a boom. Mindfulness is neither attention nor respect, nor is it appreciation or affection; it's a mysterious Fifth Element that capitalizes on its own mystery. Empathy, which is believed to be not quite the same thing as either sympathy or love, nor as justice or equity, has gained similar kudos. Values inflation takes place because, as models for living diversify, values are in a constant state of onward diversification and differentiation.

If you say values inflation, you might really mean moral inflation. This is a related, but not identical, phenomenon—that in the contemporary world we're always and everywhere challenged to make moral judgements. The media landscape requires every consumer to be constantly making moral verdicts about things that aren't really relevant to them (about civil war in South Sudan, territorial demands in the South China Sea, fracking in Texas), and in which they lack any specific expertise, for example political, ecological, economic, or military matters, because the events don't affect them. Morality is the means for creating a link to areas that don't actually have much to do with me. Moral judgements are the only judgements that modern people trust themselves to make over every conceivable object. Morality seems like the great binder—the agent for putting incompatible things in relationship with one another. And it's even the agent for justifying this putting-in-relationship. At its core, the media that reports to us on the goings-on in the various parts of the world feeds on curiosity, from love of sensation—but that's no justification for providing us with all these sensations. So morality has to be brought in, and on an industrial scale. Including in those areas where globalization does actually make us all involved. The production conditions of T-shirts in Bangladesh, of natural gas in Russia or of platinum in South Africa are indeed highly relevant to us. By means of moral judgements—ideally passed in such a way as to indict these production conditions without having any impact on our own consumption behavior—we take ourselves out of the economic responsibility cycle and transpose our new insights into the level of consequence-free indignation.

Perhaps, however, the expression "moral inflation" isn't an ideal term for the described phenomenon of a comprehensive spread of moral judgment, because morality gains value rather than losing it and, in any case, it might be too easily mixed up with values inflation. Perhaps we should instead speak of a moral boom, thus implying the next moral bust may also be on its way—for example, if *Realpolitik* once again becomes a desirable asset. We can see this happening in the nineteenth century, when "our national interests" gradually came to the fore in the media's production of a public, while moralization was the most brilliant and effective weapon both of Enlightenment figures like Voltaire (1694–1778) and of the Enlightenment anti-Enlightenment figures like Jean-Jacques Rousseau (1712–1778) for attacking the binding power of the political-theological-economical complex in the Ancien Régime (ultimately, morality did defeat might, but during the French Revolution this morality imploded into a virtues terror). Moralization is an ideal instrument for political delegitimization of others and for political self-legitimization.

By the way, moral inflation or the morals boom doesn't run synchronously with the development of the mass media, even if it might look that way if you assume that morality and publicity are closely connected. At first, the expansion of the newspapers in the nineteenth century wasn't necessarily accompanied by increases in moralizing, just as the popularization of home radios in the 1930s wasn't. You could assume the morals boom would go hand-in-hand with an increase in vocal and confident moralizing: Critical publicity makes its voice heard, distinctly, on every possible thing. If we take this vocal moral confidence seriously, albeit without prematurely draping it in laurels, we'll undeniably find that ever more people—see Internet 2.0—are speaking up and daring to join in the discussion. Admittedly, that's not in itself a proof of moral progress or of a greater readiness to engage in moral reflection. Nevertheless, morality is certainly part of the armory of those who otherwise have nothing to say. It's applicable everywhere and displaces all other criteria. That could be seen in the example of the Greek debt crisis or the "refugee crisis." When all economic and political arguments have been exhausted, the last resort turns out to be doling out verdicts of moral perfection and moral reprehensibility on all sides.

The morals boom, like other booms, gives rise to typical signs of prosperity: Once old needs are met, new needs appear; the satisfaction of needs entails the emergence and heightening of new needs. This applies to moral needs too. It wasn't so long ago that a member of the less privileged social classes could count themselves lucky not to be at constant risk of life and limb, to have had their need for physical integrity met. Today, by contrast, every individual in every social class has the moral need for psychological integrity, proudly and indignantly spurning every derogatory or insulting word as an injury to this need. So if the first moral needs are met, the next are immediately demanded, in the form of rights. No longer solely elementary and high school education for everyone, but also college education. Human rights not just for people of all genders, but also for all primates, for all life forms capable of suffering. The market of morals, like every other free market, obeys the logic of ever-increasing needs. For the observer, the question is simply: When do we reach *peak morality*, when the climb is over and the level of moral need has nowhere else to go but—more or less steeply—down?

Moral inflation and the morals boom mustn't be confused with values inflation, but values inflation is directly related to this boom. The proliferation of moral needs requires the proliferation of values. If these new, differentiated, and heightened moral needs didn't exist, maybe no one would have come up with mindfulness and empathy.

And provided we leave the torture implements of cultural pessimism in the bedside cabinet (easily to hand for another occasion), there's no need to object to values inflation. A proliferation of values refines our access to reality and our modeling of reality, which stimulates the general moral economy. In this function, values inflation is no different from economic inflation, which, by producing a proliferation of monetary values at the same time as ensuring their general loss of value, stimulates investment readiness (as well as the demand to accumulate material assets). The sober observer of the history of morality can surely only approve of the goal pursued by the European Central Bank under Mario Draghi: avoid deflation at all costs, for values as for currencies.

Values deflation, the contraction of a colorful and broad values repertoire to just a handful of values, maybe even just a single indivisible and incontrovertible good, is the normal path taken by modern societies on their way to totalitarianism. Values diversity is continuously degraded until there's suddenly just a single value—for example, the race. The rise of National Socialism makes an instructive case study of such a values deflation. In the Nazi ideology, incidentally, the terms "value" and especially "low value" (*Minderwertigkeit*), "non-value" (*Unwert*), and "valuelessness" (*Wertlosigkeit*) were leaned on heavily—and not just when Hitler lamented "how the racial degradation brings down the last Aryan values of our German people,"[1] or wanted the army to be seen as the "greatest value factor" in times of decline.[2] Occasionally the Nazi values rhetoric grasps at an idea that could be heard from quite different tendencies both before and after 1945: "The Movement must promote the respect of the person with all means necessary; it must never forget that in the personal value lies the value of all that is human,"[3] because "[i]t sees not only the different values of the races but also the different values of individual people."[4] Nonetheless, as moral deflation ran its course and the Nazis established their dictatorship, everything was ultimately subjected to the one value of racial purity—as if human beings were poodles or stud bulls.

This is where the problem of *peak morality* comes in. If the heightening of moral needs goes hand-in-hand with values inflation, while inflationary processes simultaneously tend towards being finite processes, how can we prevent the onset of a deflation that destroys the diversity? The diverse and many-voiced multiplicity of values is what saves us from any supposed tyranny of values, which only genuinely becomes a tyranny when a single value is in charge. Like a small child, every value wants undivided attention. And yet adults, their hands full with values and small children, always have to pay attention to the whole brood.

Multiplication, diversity and many-voicedness lead to *isostheneia*, to an equal strength of values. "The more values there are, the more difficult it is to see how to decide."[5] Contradictory values come to seem of equal weighting, so that any choice between them becomes arbitrary, unless you completely remove yourself from the choice and mimic the Pyrrhonist sage who refuses to make any judgment and any decision. Regardless of these individual-ethical reasonings, the sober observer will also find herself thinking: the more values, the fewer normative compulsions. While every value raises claims to validity—it's in these that its *how*, among other things, exists—it doesn't have obligating power. It functions more like an emphatic recommendation. And if there are several, numerous, indeed countless values in play, the polyphony easily escalates into a cacophony in which the individual voice can no longer be heard. The individual recommendations for action lose their emphatic force in the values heap—just as a single purchase recommendation loses its emphatic force in the advertising heap. In fact, value and advertising have more in common than the card-carrying values ontologist would be comfortable admitting. Just as advertising doesn't exert a compulsion to consume, value doesn't exert a compulsion to act.

The isosthenization of values pluralizes morality into morals. Isosthenization easily slides into apatheticization, with the result that *peak morality* can be reached more quickly than is comfortable for either the values ontologist or the sober observer. Over the course of the morals boom, rights also multiply alongside values—human rights, for example, which in their abundance and diversity likewise lose their power to exert compulsion. Or if that's not the case, to whom do I demand fulfillment of my right to paid work and my right to the best achievable state of health, as due to me pursuant to the International Covenant on Economic, Social, and Cultural Rights?

In contrast to a society with totalitarian tendencies, in which plural values are melted down into a single value, in a so-called free society the diversity and polyphony of values isn't seen as lamentable or even a necessary evil—in fact it is itself a major good, because diversity and polyphony guarantee freedom. Freedom consists significantly in polyphony and diversity. And by freedom, I mean here not a value but an empirical fact: as that which obtains when diversity and polyphony are permitted.

Admittedly, this freedom provokes regulation. And it's here that the real dilemma of freedom in the so-called free society lies. The more freedoms enjoyed by individuals and individual groups, the harder it seems to define political and even economic commonalities. Under freedom, doesn't everyone just do whatever they want, thus removing themselves from the community and, perhaps even worse, from the shared consumption of goods that are important for an economy? With a certain degree of inevitability, therefore, the expansion of freedoms provokes a greater density of regulation. More and more laws are passed with the aim of setting frameworks for more and more freedoms. The proliferation of things and the proliferation of freedoms are accompanied, therefore, not just by the proliferation of values but also by the proliferation of restrictions. We can presume that these parallel inflations won't last forever. What comes at the end?

A significant part of the *how* of values is that they're intended to *apply*. But application depends on the circumstances. Something might apply under particular conditions, in a particular framework for something or someone. Newton's law of gravitation applies for macrophysical bodies with sufficient mass density and sufficiently low velocity. Human rights apply only for members of the species *homo (sapiens?)*, but not for members of the species *felis* or the species *canis*. A human rights lawyer will quickly assert that human rights might specifically be rights for people, not cats or dogs, but they apply *universally*, and aren't attached to any conditions whatsoever. Clearly, that can't be meant as a historical truth-claim, since human rights have self-evidently not applied to all people at all times; it's only in the recent past that they've been formulated—discovered? invented?—and put into circulation. What the human rights lawyer wants to say is this: Human rights *should* apply to everybody; they apply "in principle" for all people—even people who don't know that they do. While the physicist will have no problem with the statement that the law of gravitation only applies under certain conditions, the human rights lawyer finds a similar admission decidedly difficult. Just the mention of it makes him suspect relativizers at work and, behind them, the enemies of human dignity. The problem is that human rights, in contrast to the law of gravitation, have moral values decisions deposited within them—for example, decisions about the fundamental equality and equal rights of all members of the species, or about the fundamental difference between members of this species and members of others. It's not just values that claim validity. So, for example, does positive, codified law. Naturally, the German Criminal Code and the Municipal Cemetery Ordinance are supposed to apply equally, but only for the period from the date of their entry into force until their next revision, and only for particular people under particular conditions—for criminals in Germany or for gravediggers in this city but not the one down the road. This codified law is much more than just an emphatic recommendation; it's enforced by penalty. Nonetheless, its scope remains restricted; neither the German Criminal Code nor the Municipal Cemetery Ordinance are intended to apply "universally." Positive law remains particular.

A physicist who's taken the general theory of relativity to heart will say the same of Newton's law of gravitation, because it only applies to particular physical objects. She might make use of the formulation that the law of gravitation "applies" to these objects. But application here means something different than with codified law: The objects aren't compelled by a law to attract each other on pain of a harsh penalty if they fail to comply. What "law" means here is a generalized hypothesis on the behavior of particular objects that is to be treated as true until further notice. These objects don't behave the way they behave because the law of gravitation commands them to behave that way. This "law" is in fact nothing more than a generalized description of how these objects actually behave—in all cases thus far observed, hence "law."

So the *how* of values significantly includes a claim to validity that differs from the claim to validity made by the "laws" of the natural sciences and the claim to validity made by positive law. The claim to validity made by an economic value also remains restricted and conditional; it remains particular. This house is economically valuable provided it's in a reasonable state of repair, provided there are potential buyers, provided private property is even allowed in the first place. But for the group of values that trade under the name "moral values," things seem to be fundamentally different. They seem to make a claim to universality beyond all "normal," particular validity. Notably, it seems, moral values (or their proponents) want to transcend to a world of noncontingency. To this end, the particular contingency of these moral values—the circumstances under which they were thought of and propounded—is made to disappear. If you formulate a claim of universal validity for a value, you're trying to free it from its conditions and to argue that both its emergence and its validity are unbound from any conditions. Perhaps the card-carrying values ontologist will find it easy to think of such a noncontingent thing. But the impartial observer has more work to do. Even if she accepts the existence or even the universal validity of such noncontingent values, she'll end up in difficulties if she wants to understand how something that is itself noncontingent should be a contingency for something else, for example, values-compliant actions. Surely a noncontingent thing must belong to a completely different domain of being, one where there's nothing upon which the noncontingent is contingent but, by the same token, nothing which is contingent upon the noncontingent? Hesitantly, the observer asks if the (still universal) validity claim of moral values, which is the claim to determine other things—maxim formulation, actions, forms of life—cancels itself out insofar as these values are taken out of the domain in which there is determining and contingency—in which there is causality?

The card-carrying values ontologist will suavely assure the sober observer that the old principle, that genesis and validity have nothing to do with each other, still applies. The circumstances of a particular value's discovery have no influence on how, where, and for whom it should apply. The observer won't be able to partially withhold her recognition of this principle. She agrees that the concrete circumstances in which a value emerges don't prejudice the scope or range of the validity. If a value first emerged, for example, in a Christian fundamentalist milieu, it in no way follows that it can or should apply only to Christian fundamentalists. It's entirely clear to the observer that the contexts in which a value emerged and is valid are two quite different realms. But in both realms it's the same as-if substance that matters—the value in question in the same world. In this description, the value emerges in one realm and makes its effects felt in another realm, where it is to apply. But if we claim, like the card-carrying values ontologist, that the value is not contingent but has merely been discovered, we're not simply and straightforwardly distinguishing between two realms within the same world; we're making the value into an enigmatic citizen of two worlds. The value, itself noncontingent and thus, of necessity, not having emerged into being, is at home in a higher metaphysical world but then descends, like a Greek god, from this world of the noncontingent into the world of the contingent, where it suddenly starts making all kinds of things happen—contingently. Even without being a metaphysician, you might tend towards classifying certain entities, for example numbers, as located likewise in such a world of the noncontingent. But numbers don't descend and start determining things. Their presence in the world of the contingent is not that of as-if substances but at most that of characteristics. Numbers aren't some Janus-headed twofold thing with one face in the world of the noncontingent and another in the world of the contingent.

The sober observer is exasperated. For her, values don't just have validity. Values also have history. And that makes it more than doubtful that they should be noncontingent. Admittedly, the card-carrying values ontologist, who believes in the two-worldedness of values, could also recount a history of values. It would only be the history from, as it were, the moment of incarnation, starting on the date when a value is discovered in this dismal contingent world, and extending to the ramifications of its furthest effects, of its power of validity. But these are values that pre-exist earthly history, with an eternal being in the world of the noncontingent before their power of validity in the world of the contingent. Because there's not supposed to be any becoming-contingent or being-contingent in the world of the noncontingent, there will also be no history there. The concept of validity implies, however, that effect is possible. And that's also why, to the card-carrying values ontologist, so much depends on values: Because they have an effect. It's just that, unfortunately, the values can't have any effect in the world of the noncontingent, since everything there is outside all contingency and thus resistant to all effects. In other words: Values can only have the thing that significantly makes them what they are, that's to say validity, in the world of the contingent, in the historical world.

The sober observer can imagine validity only as historical validity. Value is only value insofar as it applies in history, in the realm of the contingent. In the realm of the noncontingent, the value would not be a value, would have no validity. And to the observer, the obvious thing to do is to treat values like other mental or psychological phenomena that haven't always had their being and their validity, because they too enjoy right of residence in a world of the noncontingent. Values are contingent and made. To say so is to take two tiresome problems that tend to enrage the values-lovers and make them evaporate into thin air. Firstly, the problem of the "naturalistic fallacy." In the opinion of many ethics experts, this is something we fall into when we extrapolate what ought to be from what is. And values are indeed thought up in order to formulate an *ought*; like codified legal clauses they are made in order to apply. In neither case—legal clauses nor values—is there any mysterious jump from *be* to *ought to be*. They are what they are insofar as they demand validity. Secondly, the problem of the irreconcilable contradiction between fundamental moral values. If values are made and contingent and not based in some world of the noncontingent, it's very possible that mutually exclusive moral values with equally universal claims coexist alongside each other, having simply been produced by various people under various conditions. For some among us, for example, the fundamental equality of all people is the supreme value, while others postulate fundamental inequality as the supreme value. For the sober observer, the mere fact that such incompatible values coexist is a strong indicator of the contingency, the historical made-ness, of these values. Admittedly, this observation doesn't release the observer from the validity claims that the values (or their proponents) confront her with. She still has to react to them.

Values are to a significant extent historical—they become historically and they take effect historically. That seems to be a fault, because historicity implies changeableness and finiteness: "values are as unstable as the forms of clouds. The things that possess them are exposed to all the contingencies of existence."[6] Values are determined by contingency and appreciation—and appreciation is always the expression of a particular point of view, a particular perspective: There's no "objective appreciation" (equality is appreciated by some, while others prefer inequality). From this it follows that the *how* of values includes the state of flow, the constant shifting, emerging, and collapsing of borders and centers. This *how* is wherever possible concealed in the values discourse around moral values, in contrast, for example, to the economic values, where it's a self-evident and daily experience. In economic life, values don't mutually exclude each other; they're not in a state of direct antagonism in the way that Max Weber and Carl Schmitt imagine the relationship of moral values. Economic values are, rather, the expression of the estimation of a good, simply quantified depending on supply and demand—no matter how tirelessly the more philosophically minded economists have speculated about the "true value" of goods. So long as there's no planned economy, these values are subject to constant fluctuations. By contrast, fluctuation isn't supposed to apply to morals; the language game of morality draws its sustenance from the dogma of absoluteness. In the economic domain, therefore, values are primarily made liquid, while in the moral iteration of values they're turned to stone—or at least that's the dearly held wish. And if someone else should come along with the suspicion that values are just a cheap import to the moral realm, shiny beads from the hard world of business, you could retort that moral values are probably a kind of reversed mimicry. They disguise themselves as the harmless kind of values familiar from economics; outwardly they purport to be modern and flexible while internally they shield a concrete-encased absolutism of the good. But this reverse mimicry is ultimately nothing more than the sweet, pious wish of the card-carrying values ontologist. Observing these moral values in the natural habitat of their cultural existence, we might hear much about their diamond-hard absoluteness, but we feel and see nothing of it.

The only opportunity for long-term observation of values is provided by history—and history shows that moral values are as malleable as wax. You might think that the self-enlightening modern human would perceive this malleability by no means as a fault but in fact a major evolutionary advantage of values. To remain in the same metaphorical zone: Values made from wax burn brightly, while diamond-hard values attract desire but remain thoroughly useless in day-to-day life. Values are historical and have historical effects. Historicity is the precondition for their being and their validity.

Once you've become familiar with the idea that values are historical and that they apply historically, you've taken a major step towards the insight that our reality and, indeed, our selves are just as historical and thus changeable and finite. But the point here is not to educate ourselves into historically self-aware personhood. The point is simply that historical change is an implicit part of the values concept, so no one should be surprised by "values change." It's not just that values are historical; the value of values is also historical (Ève-Lyne Perron). If, as is often claimed, values are collapsing, then this needs to be contrasted with the emergence of new values. The *how* of values is, substantially, mutability.

If you ask about the *how* of values, you're also asking about their type and nature, how they really are. It should be clear that the answers from the card-carrying values ontologist don't really help us here. Clinging stubbornly to an alternative between being and not-being, to the old fiction of Parmenides (c. 520–460 BCE) that still impresses, or oppresses, some philosophers, will get us nowhere.[7] There are clearly diverse levels and grades of being real,[8] types and nuances of existing; there's not simply being or not being. Unicorns and visions have their reality too, even if presumably not so densely as the reality of the value "equality" or the reality of the trash basket under my desk, to which I consign many of my almost-realities. There are infinite possibilities for something to exist—and for how something can exist. The *how*-ness of earthly things, which include values, is irrevocably a temporariness.

Instead of the *how*, we speak today using the technical word *mode*—perhaps nerds are craftily engaging in a sneaky cult of Spinoza? For Baruch de Spinoza (1632–1677) there was only one substance, one that had multiple modes. In any case, computers don't have periods, they have modes, such as airplane mode, quiet mode, and energy-saving mode. Do values also have their modes? What do they do when they're in their modes? Is the contemporary world so intent on values because they're generally in sleep mode? Or are values themselves the energy-saving mode of the good? Once again I note that provisionality is the unmistakable mark of values.

Notes

1. Adolf Hitler: Mein Kampf. Zwei Bände in einem Band. Ungekürzte Ausgabe. Munich 1943, p. 621.
2. ibid., p. 305.
3. ibid., p. 387.
4. ibid., p. 421.
5. Niklas Luhmann: Die Gesellschaft der Gesellschaft. Frankfurt a. M. 1997, vol. 2, p. 800.
6. John Dewey: Experience and Nature. London 1929, p. 399.
7. See Ludger Lütkehaus: Nichts. Abschied vom Sein. Ende der Angst. Revidierte Neuausgabe. Leipzig 2014, pp. 612–615.
8. See Paul Feyerabend: The Conquest of Abundance: A Tale of Abstraction versus the Richness of Being ed. Bert Terpstra, Chicago and London 1999.

CHAPTER 4

The Power to Connect, the Power to Relativize. What Do Values Relate To?

Abstract Some argue that values relate only within the discourse of values and not to the external world. These values are seen as existing in a sea of indistinguishable multiplicity. Values emerge from an evolutionary history that involved comparison and differentiation. Immanuel Kant posited the notion of dignity as inner value, inseparable from moral ability. However, the absoluteness of values raises questions, leading to moral absolutism. Values exist in relation to each other, forming a network of relationships. Moral absolutism clashes with values thought, and the debate extends to the relationship between values and individuals. Are values dependent on humans, or are humans dependent on values? This chapter explores the dynamic and complex interplay between values and their connections, highlighting the relativity that underpins their existence.

Keywords Relativization • Connection • Dignity • Comparison • Emergence • Self-concept • Preferences • Absolutism • Relationships

Once upon a time, when values were still leading a humble existence as mere accidents, everything was simpler: They related purely to whatever they were tacked onto. "Value" was one of the characteristics that could be attributed to an object alongside such characteristics as being big, being green, or being patient. Today, by contrast, the first answer to the question of what values relate to is … values.

A. U. Sommer, *Values*,
https://doi.org/10.1007/978-3-031-42159-4_4

There are even some malcontents who, far from disagreeing, would double down: Values, they say, relate only to each other within values discourse, not to anything out there, "as if there were a thousand bars and behind those thousand bars no world."[1] Values, they claim, vegetate in a values sea, an oily values swamp, indistinguishable from each other, never alone but always in multiples. And if you dive in for a swim, the putrid odor will stay on your skin for weeks. No, not the sharp odor of Rainer Maria Rilke's (1875–1926) caged panther, pacing behind those thousand bars in Paris's *Jardin des plantes*, but that of a gangrenous body.

"Why did no one ever tell me about the odor of values?" says the sober observer to the values malcontent, "One meets them in the flesh so seldom, it's enough to doubt they really exist." In fact, however, a community-forming tendency seems to be inherent to values. Wherever one value is, there will usually be others not far away. This social behavior of the as-if substances called "values" is explained by their evolutionary history. In an earlier stage of development, when values were still only characteristics, they were of necessity compared against each other. If you ascribed value to a piece of rock because a silver vein ran through it, you did so in comparison with the ore-less rubble scattered valuelessly on the slag heap. If you ascribed value to tulip bulbs because you had a thing for tulips, you did so in comparison with potato tubers, which you weren't that bothered about. If you use "value" as an accident, you do so to distinguish something in comparison with something else, to differentiate it according to the level of your appreciation. Something is valuable if I compare it with another thing and find it better. Accordingly, even in Roman times, the price and value of a thing flowed together into one word, *pretium*. The Middle Ages put the expression *valor*, "value," into circulation to mean the right price, *iustum pretium*, thus shifting to a distinction between the true, inner value of a thing and the price that's actually paid for it.

In his *Groundwork of the Metaphysics of Morals* of 1785, Immanuel Kant (1724–1804) argues that in the "realm of ends" everything has "either a price or a dignity. What has a price is such that something else can also be put in its place as its equivalent; by contrast, that which is elevated above all price, and admits no equivalent, has a dignity."[2] For Kant, dignity is the same thing as "inner value"—it's that "which makes up the condition under which alone something can be purpose in itself."[3] So there's nothing else that can take the place of dignity or inner value—dignity is an end in itself—while things that have been priced are capable of mutual substitution. At the same time, "morality is the sole condition under which a reasonable being can be a purpose in itself, because it is only through reason that it is possible to be a lawmaking member in the realm of ends." Kant's endeavor is thus to carve out, from the realm of equivalent substitution in which everything has its price, an enclave in which purpose in itself rules—a morality that doesn't aim at "advantage and benefit" but expresses itself "in the sentiments, i.e. in the maxims of the will." For Kant, dignity or inner value is something indissolubly connected to moral ability, the capacity for self-legislation—mere belonging to the zoological category of human being, for example, is in no way grounds for dignity in his sense. But Kant's reason puts this dignity "infinitely beyond all price, against which it cannot by any means be brought into account or comparison without injury to the sanctity of the same."[4] We note the intention but something doesn't seem right. Dignity, inner value, and morality should be immunized at all costs against the attempt to put them into comparative relations with each other, to put price tags on them, weigh them up against extra- or non-moral considerations. Clearly, Kant's own strategy of metaphysical immunization seemed so weak to him that he had to draw on religious tabooization: "Holiness" is no argument but a primitive means of silencing objections.

The notion that dignity or inner value should remain permanently exempted from the drive to compare seems doubtful. Correlativity has permanently embedded its accidental forebears into the evolutionary history of the as-if substance called "values." Values, even when conceived as substances, are values in comparison with other values. In the quoted passage, Kant only avoids having to conceive values in relation to other values by trying to deny this constraint with a metaphor of surpassing. Dignity, he says, is "endlessly put away beyond all price." Well, you're welcome to believe that if you want to. But Kant's victory in the battle of metaphors isn't elevated above all doubt. Values exist in reference to other values. Whatever values are, they are in relation. In the days of mere values accidents, a thing was more or less valuable than another thing, but values that are conceived as substantial must be measured with others of their kind. Something is a value in comparison with other values. An "absolute value" that can't be compared with other values would be a thing that (as with all absolutes) a person wouldn't know what to do with. They couldn't operationalize this "absolute value;" they couldn't place it in a relationship with either their non-absolute actions, their non-absolute life, or with non-absolute values. An "absolute value" from the world of the noncontingent would be a "non-thing" that had nothing to do with human beings, because absoluteness applies to nothing and accomplishes nothing in a contingent world.

Values prove themselves in comparison with other values. They stand in relationship to them—even if only a relationship of mutual exclusion. The value of equality stands in just such a relationship of mutual exclusion with the value of inequality. The value of freedom and the value of security don't exclude each other, but they can compete with each other depending on how they're weighted. The diversity of values, their irreducibility to a single supposed über-value, brings with it their relativity. Freedom, for example, isn't a value that applies under all possible circumstances unconditionally; like any other value, it has its limits. Some of these limits are other values, including, of course, the value of security. To talk of values is to acknowledge their mutual relativization and their relativity. If we were to undertake an "unprejudiced" investigation of values, we'd "quickly be persuaded of the relativity even of ethical and aesthetic values. Nothing is valuable or valueless from nature; people make it so."[5] As unwilling as card-carrying values ontologists may be to hear this, relativity is inevitably implanted in values thought. Relativism means thinking of reality as a network of relationships.

For that reason, moral absolutism tends to cherish a decided antipathy to values thought. A positively archetypal example of this is Albert Schweitzer (1875–1965), who in 1931 accused the values philosophies of the inter-war years of engaging in an "endeavor to lay down universally valid value differences between living beings" with the aim of "judging them on the basis of whether they seem to be closer to or further from us humans according to our perception, which is a subjective measure." "Then, depending on the circumstances, species of insects or primitive peoples can be understood as valueless life."[6] As a critique of the objectivism of certain moth-eaten values philosophies, this complaint is doubtless justified. The critique is based on an absolute ethics that he had already formulated in 1923 in *Kultur und Ethik*: "The ethic of awe in the face of life recognizes no relative ethics. The only good it allows to apply is the preservation and support of life. It defines all destruction and damage to life, regardless of the circumstances in which it may take place, as evil."[7] Whatever a person does, they must decide, and they will inevitably incur guilt, because they will impair other lives in the course of their own life. "The good conscience is an invention of the devil."[8] Having found fault with values and suspecting that values philosophies must of necessity be relativist, Schweitzer returns resolutely to the moral absolutism of good and evil.

It's notable, incidentally, that the thesis that life is the supreme value has gained widespread political acceptance in our own time—albeit limited to human life. In debates about euthanasia and assisted dying, for example, both proponents and objectors regard the value of this human life as equally absolute, which shows that life is no longer something that one can or must assign a value to.[9] Can or should people choose to die? For many, even to consider this question from the perspective of what a person might still be able to offer a society, and thus of what their value to it is, is to subject human life to a sinister capitalist logic of exploitation. But it's not quite that. That point is reached when one urges people to take their own lives because they're old and sick and no longer of "use" to anyone. Rather, if you claim that life is a value in itself—"value of life" is a formula put into circulation in 1792 by Friedrich Ernst Daniel Schleiermacher (1768–1834) and popularized by Eugen Dühring (1833–1921)[10]—you've put yourself in the service of the capitalist logic, which is a logic of values, of value exchange. To absolutize a particular value can't do much to change this logic, in which there are in principle no absolute values, in which, rather, all values are negotiable. If you're talking about values at all, the rot has already set in. Life as the supreme value is a value of desperation, because otherwise there's no way of reaching values consensus in the values pluriverse. But who requires such a consensus, if values are necessarily relative and relational?

As unwilling as the card-carrying values ontologist may be to admit it, Schweitzer correctly observed that taking values thought to its logical conclusion leads to relativism, because values can't be sustainably stabilized in a historical world. But to use this as a pretext for returning, like Schweitzer, to a long-since worn-out metaphysical idol like the good-in-itself? That can't be the solution either. Instead, despite the neo-Kantian appearance of objectivism in earlier values philosophies, their present-day potential lies in particular in their dynamism, their mutability. Temporariness is the promise of a modern values philosophy—temporariness of its values, but probably also temporariness of this values philosophy itself. In relation among each other, values take part in a permanent elimination contest; in the diversity of values, one gets the better of the other, while a third, despite bringing up the rear, long maintains its small squad of devotees trailing behind it. At the same time, there are clearly also divergences between the de facto and the verbal validity of a value. The value of freedom, for example, seems to have been displacing a plethora of other values from the general values discourse for centuries—outside of churches and other confessional special interest groups, for example, who still speaks of brotherly love?—even as the de facto validity of it doesn't look quite so rosy. Which value asserts itself most powerfully—and under which conditions—is seldom easy to assess with any certainty. It's often impossible, or will only become possible in the distant future, for the observer to know which is the value that proved the fittest to survive.

Values—insofar as they are to be more than airy visions, by which I mean absolute and thus non-existent entities—relate to other values. But not just to other values: also, for example, to people and their interests. The card-carrying values ontologist will define the relationship thus: Persons relate to values. Persons are dependent on values to be able to live. Human beings are values-dependent beings.

If you don't share the ardent faith of the values ontologist, you might want to reverse the relationship: Values relate to persons. In order for values to apply, they're dependent on persons—persons who recognize them as well as persons who create them in the first place. Without people there are no values. Values are human-dependent beings, if they are beings at all. In his 1897 volume of essays *The Will to Believe,* the pragmatist William James (1842–1910) pointed out that things like morals and values could only exist in a universe in which feeling creatures prefer particular situations to other situations and in which there is the possibility of sensation.[11] Values need a habitat, and their habitat is that of the sensing creature. "Neither moral relations nor the moral law can swing *in vacuo.* Their only habitat can be a mind which feels them; and no world composed of merely physical facts can possibly be a world to which ethical propositions apply."[12] According to this concept, values belong to the conditions of human interaction, which admittedly doesn't give them any special status among these conditions. For the pragmatist, our understanding of the world, our reality in its entirety, is socially formed and calibrated to our shared options for action. Values—and even the non-pragmatist could admit this—are in our human interest.

Today's pragmatists go further when, like Hans Joas (b. 1948), they try to investigate "how values connection emerges".[13] The expression "values connection" might appeal to the card-carrying values ontologist because it evokes an association that values exist somehow before individuals, who then decide to bind themselves to these pre-existing things. Something like this might well be the case for the individual, born into a community that is already defined by values (or believes itself to be), but it doesn't have anything to say about the genesis of values themselves, which may very well still be subject to negotiation—in fact to a succession of renegotiations, as young people grow to maturity. But if you enquire directly into values connection, you might be tempted to sweepingly ignore the much more fundamental point of values emergence. Emergence must, logically, precede connection—provided values are a thing that emerges. Certainly, Joas speaks emphatically of the emergence of values: "Values emerge in experiences of self-formation and self-transcendence."[14] Values are clearly something entirely exceptional and incomparable with the rest of our reality, since their emergence is the "core of human experience."[15] It remains obscure, however, how experience can have a "core." There may be different intensities of experience, but experience, in contrast to apples, planets, and nuclear reactors, doesn't seem to contain a core, unless one wanted to suggest that there was something behind experience, that is, the thing one has experience of, perhaps a descendent of the thing-in-itself. In brief: Are values now aspects of experience, perhaps socially constructed aspects of experience, or even something that precedes all experience? Nevertheless, here we're being expressly told that values "emerge in experiences," and moreover in specific experiences of "self-formation and self-transcendence"—so they're posited neither in the sense of the card-carrying values ontologist nor in the sense of a social *a priori*. It seems as if values-genesis and self-genesis run in parallel—and as if the social dimension, via a non-religious concept of "self-transcendence" joins in. If you want to restock your values-philosophical armory with neo-pragmatist ammunition, you also need to buy in a lot of self-metaphysics. Because it's clear that the concept of the self weighs much more heavily here than the feather-light self we're so quick to invoke in day-to-day life. It's associated with realness, with authentic identity—with that which in reality comprises us.

For the sober observer, this kind of authentic self is hard to digest, and not just because she mistrusts Last Things and thus also sees the authentic self vanishing like mist (perhaps that could be counted as self-transcendence). What will intuitively trouble her even more about this notion is that it lends values an accentuated, unique meaning that distinguishes them from all the other things (including thoughts, sensations, theories) that hominids have to deal with. Why should values, of all things, be linked in such a significant way with the ominous self or with the "core of human experience"—much more so than interests, thoughts, sensations? Perhaps, in order to be able to emerge or apply, values don't need any selves at all, just evaluating lifeforms. A values interpretation that does without an ambitious self-concept might be more congenial to the Korean philosopher Kal Choi (b. 1978). For him, values are purposes that go back to the will of the evaluator and significantly also depend on the strength of this will. It's easy to lose sight, here, of the fact that values are not usually things that we directly attempt to reach; as commonly understood, it's more the case that they're what pushes us to strive for particular aims in the first place. The purpose of my *action* may be to rescue the man who's just fallen into the river, but it will be something like the *value* of life or of the protection of human dignity that guided me towards doing so. According to this habit of speaking and thinking, values determine our goal-setting because they pre-form our preferences.

So values stand in relation to our preferences. But how should we conceive this relationship? For Georg Henrik von Wright (1916–2003) values are "unconditional preferences,"[16] while Rudolf Carnap (1891–1970) describes them as value attitudes that express a permanent desire: "Therefore, I shall use the Latin word 'utinam'; 'utinam *p*' (where any declarative sentence may be substituted for '*p*') to mean approximately the same as 'wish that *p*' or 'would that *p*'."[17] In these expositions, the relationship of value and preference is that of identity. Here we understand preference as a wish made permanent, as a wish-attitude. If you have difference-philosophical difficulties with identities, you might see the preference, the habitually sedimented wish, as also being the source of values, in which preferences manifest themselves as regulative variables for the purpose of practical life application. But a difference philosopher could not want to reverse this postulated difference solely on account of the difference. Values would then be the source of preferences; they would be wish-production machines.

So if you map out the possible value-preference relationships without prior assumptions, you get a colorful and varied panorama, depending on the perspective you choose. Either values beget preferences or are begotten by preferences—or the two are coextensive. Now, a philosopher who understood herself as a lawmaker could pass off one or another of these possible relationships as the sole, unique, and correct one, and dismiss all the others as incorrect. Anyone can pronounce any kind of decree they like, but reality doesn't always follow these decrees, especially not the ones that come from philosophers. Perhaps there is some kind of vagueness relationship between the complementary variables "value" and "preference," like that postulated by quantum mechanics as applying between the momentum and position of an elementary particle. The more precisely I can define one of the two variables, the less precise the other remains. By contrast, if you insist that you can definitively gauge both variables and their relationship to each other, you're following a political values agenda. You might demonstrate, for example, that values initially justify preferences or that values are justified by preferences. Unfortunately, each of these demonstration processes assumes something that remains to be proved. In each case, what is shown isn't that values "in reality" behave in such and such a way but only that there's a particular role that values play in the speaker's understanding of reality.

A similar insight can be gained from the question of how values relate to interests. Some like to equate interests to preferences—to see preferences as interests made explicit. The potential conclusions from this would be exactly as stated above. But the term "interest," as commonly understood, seems to refer more pointedly to de facto circumstances, while the term "preference" is targeted more to psychological circumstances. I might have a persistent preference for sugary drinks, even though this preference runs counter to my interests, specifically my interest in the long-term survival of my organism. Interests seem to be objectively definable, regardless of what any particular actor believes their individual inclinations are. Interests seem to constitute the granite floor of every being. If that's the case, it would seem reasonable to denounce values as the emanation of these interests or to say that anything that attracts interest must be considered a value: "*x* is valuable = interest is taken in *x*."[18] Values would then be nothing more than an elevated form of articulating or disguising interests. The speculator whose main interest is in accumulating capital will swear allegiance to the value of the free market because this seems to serve her main interest most effectively. This is where the incensed cultural critic interjects that values seem to be merely the colloquial mantra chanted by a thoroughly corrupt society to silence its enemies. Values as narcotics, their validity decided not on the basis of the better argument but on the dominance of interests. Values as inventions, devised to put interests beyond the reach of critique, to sanctify them. If the cultural critic's objection were to prove correct, then interests might not exhibit such granite immutability. And can it be that the things the cultural critic deploys against interests are in fact values?

Then there are the cases in which there seems to be a fundamental conflict between interests and values. Such cases occur when someone places values above interests and, in particular, when they're prepared to sacrifice their interests to their values. A classic example would be the revolutionary who prioritizes liberty over her own life, blowing herself up in a bomb attack on the dictator. To speak of a fundamental conflict here between interests and values is to assume that interests are objectively present and that the interest in one's own survival is the highest interest. The implication, therefore, is that interests are something fixed and that the interest in preservation of life as a biological fact takes precedence over all other interests. But this rigid model misses that interests are also formable. It's easy to imagine situations in which I place my interest in the prolonging of my life below other interests; life isn't necessarily the supreme good. For the revolutionary, her supreme value of liberty is identical with her supreme interest.

But values don't just relate to vague objects such as themselves or preferences and interests; they also relate to hard realities, like institutions for example. The revolutionary's fury—fed by values—is aimed against institutions, or at least against those that seem to stand in the way of her value of freedom. It's easy to assume that values are generally anti-institutional—that they want to destroy institutions. Note how loud the clamor for values is in the fight against globalization or in the run-up to political insurgencies!

But it's just as easy to imagine a different kind of relationship between values and institutions. Values may be made concrete in institutional form; institutions may represent particular values—just think of confessional communities or the UN's various specialist organizations. But values can also play a role in the design and formation of institutions; values can define them. This might take place via the indirect route of laws that call forth, regulate, and commission institutions. Laws have an institutionalizing and normative force; they directly form our existence. Values, by contrast, have an indefinite effect, and in contrast to some other immaterial entities, such as numbers or indeed laws, their boundaries are blurry. Nonetheless, if a society defines itself as bound by shared values, then values belong, in one way or another, in the causal chain that produces laws—as partial causes or as partial conditions for their possibility. The Germans, for example, like to ascribe their laws to the values they see as underlying the Basic Law, the country's constitution. The ways in which values determine action are often not direct—although that happens too; see the freedom-loving revolutionary—but indirect, a function of their being sedimented in laws or in social behavioral rules below the threshold of any codification. If we accept this, then we can no longer see values as living out a "salon existence" (Niklas Grouls); they can no longer merely be elderly uncles whose friendly advice we acknowledge for the sake of politeness but don't follow. In this reading, values would have a more strongly normative power than these eccentric relatives.

Doubts remain. According to this model, societies cultivate values by forming them themselves; values are then codified as laws or arranged as norms—norms understood here as binding requirements for how we live and act in community with others. "Values justify moral action—norms restrict and sanction it."[19] For the card-carrying values ontologist, the "connection of values and norms" is entirely unproblematic: "The aforementioned values obligate us to actions because it is good to realize something valuable, for the meaning of moral action is doing good and avoiding bad. It follows from this, in turn, that it is the meaning of obligating moral action which is guided by norms to contribute to the good of human beings."[20] But how values can "obligate" remains, admittedly, obscure. And if they can obligate, are they not then simply already norms? If so, we could confidently offer them up to Ockham's razor. Or is it more the case that norms are curdled values on an operational, middle level, concretizations of values for daily use? If freedom, for example, counts as a value, then would the norm not be that my exercise of freedom must not curtail the exercise of freedom by my fellow humans? But, once again, depending on the status that you grant to values (as well as norms) in your own understanding of reality and speech acts, you will verbalize the relationship differently. Instead of seeing values as norm-justifying—would a plurality of mutually contradictory norms necessarily follow from values plurality?—you could think of values as a fig leaf with which de facto applicable norms, e.g., the right to private property ownership, are merely protected and justified.

Whatever you specifically label the circumstances, it can be decisively assumed that values produce relationships. Values connect, they associate that which is unassociated. Which is why the emergence of domain-transgressing values-thought stems from the nineteenth century. In an age when convictions of religious-metaphysical work could no longer perform their binding function and the old-European fabric of thinking, believing, and feeling was breaking apart, a new cement was urgently needed.[21] Values seemed to be able to satisfy precisely this connecting interest. These are relationship fictions with the potential to put everything in connection with everything and to establish comparability. The objective ordering of things had been thrown into disarray, and now values promised to amalgamate what had become unbound. While the values philosophers of the first, second, and third waves still cherished a hope that values would help to restore the objective order of the universe, younger colleagues have parted from this pious hope. The tendency now is to recognize that it's positively because they are situative and partial—rather than "universal"—that values can perform their service as binding machines, relationship generators, and comparability guarantors.

If we stay true to the values discourse, then it's precisely because it helps us to get away from the metaphysical specter of universalism. Understood critically, values mean a departure from the absolute good. The binary code good/evil is just as much an expression of a complete impoverishment of the world as is the binary code being/not being. Values overcome such either/or distinctions by producing relationships, promoting fluidity, generating dynamism. They create many-layeredness and flexibility. And they do all this, naturally, under the condition that we act as if they existed. That which money enables in everyday social practice, values enable in the everyday practice of thinking and feeling. Values are a magic potion for putting everything into relationship with everything else.

Notes

1. Rainer Maria Rilke: Sämtliche Werke. Hg. vom Rilke-Archiv in Verbindung mit Ruth Sieber-Rilke, besorgt von Ernst Zinn. Wiesbaden/Frankfurt a. M. 1955, vol. 1, p. 505.
2. Immanuel Kant: Grundlegung zur Metaphysik der Sitten. In: idem.:Gesammelte Schriften. Hg. von der Königlich Preußischen Akademie der Wissenschaften. Abteilung 1, vol. 4. Berlin 1911, pp. 385–463, here p. 434.
3. ibid., p. 435.
4. ibid.
5. Fritz Mauthner: Wörterbuch der Philosophie. Neue Beiträge zu einer Kritik der Sprache. Munich/Leipzig 1910, vol. 2, p. 582.
6. Albert Schweitzer: Gesammelte Werke in fünf Bänden. ed. Rudolf Grabs. Zürich undated [1974], vol. 1, p. 242.
7. ibid., vol. 2, p. 387.
8. ibid., vol. 2, p. 388, cf. Albert Schweitzer/Fritz Buri: Existenzphilosophie und Christentum. Briefe 1935–1964. Introduced, annotated and ed. by Andreas Urs Sommer. Munich 2000, p. 45.

9. Natalie Schulte: Lebenslust und Leid. Nietzsche über die Selbsttötung. Masterarbeit zur Erlangung des akademischen Grades Master of Arts, Albert-Ludwigs-Universität. Freiburg im Breisgau 2015, p. 84.
10. Eugen Dühring: Der Werth des Lebens. Eine philosophische Betrachtung. Wroclaw 1865.
11. William James: The Will to Believe and Other Essays in the Popular Philosophy. New York/London/Bombay 1897, p. 189 f.
12. Ibid., p. 190.
13. Hans Joas: Die Entstehung der Werte. Frankfurt a. M. 1997, p. 16.
14. ibid., p. 10.
15. ibid., p. 23.
16. Niklas Luhmann: Die Gesellschaft der Gesellschaft. Frankfurt a. M. 1997, Bd. 1, S. 342.
17. Paul Arthur Schilpp (ed.): The Philosophy of Rudolf Carnap. La Salle, Ill. 1963, p. 1003.
18. Ralph Barton Perry: General Theory of Values. Its Meaning and Basic Principles Construed in Terms of Interest. Cambridge, Mass. 1950, p. 116.
19. Rüdiger Funiok: Medienethik. Verantwortung in der Mediengesellschaft. Stuttgart 2007, p. 47 f.
20. Detlef Horster: Das Verhältnis von Normen und Werten. In: Wilfried Härle/Bernhard Vogel (eds.):»Vom Rechte, das mit uns geboren ist«. Aktuelle Probleme des Naturrechts. Hg. im Auftrag der Konrad Adenauer-Stiftung e. V. Freiburg i. Br. u. a. 2007, pp. 202–215, here p. 210 f.
21. See Martin Heidegger: Holzwege = idem.: Gesamtausgabe. I. Abteilung:Veröffentliche Schriften 1914–1970. Frankfurt a. M. 1977, vol. 5, p. 227.

CHAPTER 5

At Home Nowhere and Everywhere. Where and When Are Values (in Use)?

Abstract The chapter delves into the intricate interplay of values within the realm of human communication and philosophy. It explores the paradoxical presence and absence of values in various contexts and timeframes. The analysis begins by challenging the notion of values' existence primarily within academic philosophy, highlighting their broader circulation beyond academia. The chapter navigates through the duality of values, examining their claim to universality, while acknowledging their particularity and contextual limitations. Drawing parallels with language, it introduces the concept of values discourse as a specific normative language, influencing interpersonal interactions and decision-making. The discourse also touches on the role of fear in shaping values and its potential impact on societies. The chapter discusses how values are invoked for legitimization, justification, and communal identity. It delves into the intricate relationship between values, pluralism, and evolving societal conditions. Throughout, the dynamic nature of values is emphasized, revealing their adaptability and potential for change in response to human interactions and contexts.

Keywords Universality • Contextual limitations • Normative language • Justification • Pluralism • Evolving societies • Fear and values • Interpersonal interactions • Adaptability

A. U. Sommer, *Values*,
https://doi.org/10.1007/978-3-031-42159-4_5

In our discussion of the *how* of values, their *where* and *when* in everyday communication situations also played an important role. A mischievous answer to the *where* and *when* of values could go something like this: somewhere else and yesterday, in any case not now and here. If you looked exclusively at the academic philosophy of continental Europe, you'd have to agree with the mischief-maker. The heyday of the formal and material values philosophies was in the last century. Values have, admittedly, survived; it's just that no professional ethicist would handle them today without protective gloves. But as soon as you widen the horizon and venture out of the academic philosophy biotope, you'll see that values are suddenly in general circulation, as if they either wanted to punish the academic philosophers' lies or were demonstrating the delayed impact of the academic philosophy of yesteryear. Without the diverse values philosophies of earlier times, values would have never gotten as far as they have in general circulation. So the *where* and *when* answer is a strange one. Philosophically and academically, values have been driven back (except for in their anglophone analytic enclave); at the same time, countless non-philosophers have started to pay homage to them. Even so, academic philosophy still has a part to play in answering the question of why that should be the case.

The *where* and *when* of de facto values-use and values-discourse are one thing. Quite another is the claim with which the values-use and values-discourse are associated: If I propagate a moral value, I want it to stay on the scene, to be valid superotemporally. So a valid answer to the question of the *where* of moral values would be: everywhere! And to the *when* question: always! So ubiquity and timelessness would be the two characteristics that should be ascribed to moral values. These characteristics follow from their claim to universality. Values should apply to everyone, to all possible persons at all times in all places. Until now, these characteristics were reserved for God. The universal claim of values, which expresses itself in the arrogated characteristics of ubiquity and timelessness, stands in strange contrast to their de facto particularity—their sobering, upsetting chronological and spatial limitedness. Unfortunately, the fact that they are claimed to be universal does not give rise to a fact that this claim corresponds to any kind of reality. The more sweeping the claim, the less probable that it will be fulfilled (which, incidentally, works the same way with goblins, yetis, unicorns, vampires, and gods).

Here the observer returns humbly to the *where* and *when* of de facto values-use and values-discourse. One potential aid here is a remark by Karl

Bühler (1879–1963) on the economy of communication, in which he notes "the general fact that what is superfluous or dispensable is left out in terse verbal contact": "The fact that there is completely mute contact between human psyches and that within this mute contact it is possible that an acoustic sign will turn up only occasionally like an island in the sea must be taken as a basis."[1] Formulated differently, language comprises islands in a sea of silence, of silent intercourse. Speaking doesn't take priority; non-speaking does. An abundance of actions and interactions can be completed without any linguistic input; language comes into play only at the moment when things can no longer be managed non-verbally. So language only becomes truly necessary in crisis situations, even if Bühler's exposition makes insufficient mention that language often enough serves not for explanation but merely for filling (often unbearable[2]) silences or for creating narrative worlds in a culture otherwise committed to well-practiced, wordless routines.[3] At all events, language is primarily neither a world-depicting machine nor an information-transfer machine.

Perhaps, therefore, we should simply identify what I've somewhat dismissively called "values discourse" as a specific language that fits into the normative syntax, the normative grammar, of human and specifically Western culture—just as Italian or Portuguese fit into the Romance language family? We could then place the *where* and *when* of values into analogy with the *where* and *when* of speaking. So speaking disambiguates self-evident processes, strips away their multiple potential interpretations. The default state is actually silence, and it's only in critical situations or to fill this silence that language articulates itself. In the same way, values are intended to disambiguate self-evident behavioral patterns. The default state that values come up against would be indifference. Values come into play when situations become so critical that they demand decisions—or a justification of decisions already made. In the latter case, we tell stories in which values play a role as influencing powers.

This thread ties up values in the web of language, and if we continue to spin it we might end up connecting the proliferation of the values discourse with the insight from cultural criticism that in modern societies things that used to be self-evident have broken down, rendering the silent intercourse dysfunctional. Has not morality—the language family to which values belong—ceased to be self-evident?

A more precise description might be that certain morality patterns that used to be self-evident within a society have stopped being self-evident. In the period between around 1850 and around 1910, the inhabitants of a village in the Black Forest would have been almost completely unanimous about the sole proper moral paradigm, with the result that discussion of morals seemed superfluous once parents had taught it to their children. The only reason for speaking of the moral paradigm again would be if someone had infringed it and thus created the need for an update. Today, by contrast, diversity has found its way into even this Black Forest village; people of varying moral provenances have settled there with the result that there is more need for *speaking* about morals. The themes now include the girls whose Muslim families don't want them to go to swimming lessons and the demand by an atheist father for the crucifix to be removed from the elementary school classroom, and as a matter of some urgency please. This newly increased need for talking about morality is, of course, no indicator of any general moral collapse. Quite the reverse, it's the expression of an attempt to use morality to regulate interpersonal relationships that previously might have been regulated simply through the threat of punishment, perhaps even of psychological and physical violence, that's to say, the law of the strongest. Deviant behavior was penalized socially. Since there's no shared, self-evident moral foundation—and the balance or imbalance of the power relations can't be assessed, leaving everyone ignorant of who would have the upper hand in a non-discursive dispute—negotiations about what ought to or must be done become necessary. And this need for moral speech tends to be fulfilled via values. Values are the legal tender in everyday moral discourse.

What values testify to and bring forth is not some general decline and moral decay but the retreat of moral indifference. We might connect this retreat, firstly, with a heightening of the moral sense, that is, not with a decline but with a general moral rearmament that subjects many areas of life that were long enough either self-evident or extra-moral to moral critique. There was a time when child labor, for example, was not a moral question, nor was the gender ratio in family and public life. Secondly, this retreat of moral indifference could be a result of the proliferation of moral situations produced by competing yet coexisting moralities.

That doesn't mean that the actual number of self-evident things has declined and that all the practicalities of life have become questionable amid the competition and coexistence of moralities. For example, almost all these competing moralities hold it an unquestionable certainty that the killing of an innocent is worthy of moral condemnation. But alongside the still-large number of moral self-evidences that there's no need to debate, a wealth of situations has arisen in our times in which different moral claims come into conflict or in which moral claims come into conflict with extra-moral (for example economic or political) demands. Modernity means diversification of lived realities; modern people no longer live in one world but in multiple worlds. There is a constant need for balancing and mediation between these worlds and between all people in their world-multiplicity; the weights and interests must be continuously balanced and rebalanced. All this happens without the number of self-evidences having declined—it's just that in contrast to some idealized "old days," there are more circumstances that can't be dealt with by self-evident routines.

The potential situations of interpersonal interaction within the scope of different moralities have multiplied and with them the potential conflicts. Which is why there is a need for morality discourse, a need that we satisfy by discussing "values" and assuring each other that whatever actions we undertake that disconcert our interlocutors are bound to "values." Instances of conflict, therefore, are interruptions to the natural indifference of the silent intercourse of moral self-evidences; we feel ourselves required to make conscious decisions. Mutually assuring each other of our commitment to values helps to numb this painful rupture. Values are reassuring, even when they fundamentally contradict each other. While they don't restore the thoughtless indifference before the eruption of a conflict, they do support the shared finding of a new indifference.

To give one example: In our Black Forest village, homosexual acts were considered self-evidently reprehensible in 1850, 1910, and 1950. Since then, this severe attitude has disappeared; today, most of the population would object just as little to gay acts as to heterosexual acts between consenting adult partners. And a decisive part of what made this change possible is a new understanding of what people call "values"—for example, the value of privacy or the value of love ("The most important thing is just to love someone …"): Homosexuality, once punished by criminal and social sanctions, stops being a moral problem where morality discourse is defined by values. In its place, discrimination against gay people becomes a moral problem because it runs counter to the values that have become predominant in the discourse.

If you enquire into the *where* and *when* of values, it's obviously not enough to point only to their conflict-assuaging role in discussions of morality. Values clearly also turn up in human communication in very different places and on very different occasions. The *where* and *when* of values tells us something about their functioning in the verbal interaction of human beings.

Values show up in this verbal interaction wherever the intention is to make morality manageable and practical for use in daily activity. If we take morality as a whole as a life-determining conception of reality, values would be the tools and machines with which this whole tends to concretely put life into action. They help us to implement a practical conception of reality on a small scale instead of staying with the generality of abstract principles.

Values surface in spoken interaction wherever there's a need for legitimization. Values are often called upon by those whose actions contradict other people's interests. A city administration invokes the value of sustainability if it decides not to build a road that would provide easier access to the shopping district and prevent massive traffic jams. In communication, therefore, values can be brought to bear against interests, which suggests that they're not simply identical with interests. The invocation of values against interests usually happens when the speaker doesn't share these interests and wants to outdo them with a higher card. Values are trumps and beat interests. But sometimes we play values against our own interests; they legitimate an action that seems to counteract our own wellbeing. Although it would serve the young economist's interests to keep the fabulously profitable arms company's shares in her portfolio, she chooses not to, because the investment contradicts her values. Values often justify a behavior that runs counter to interests.

Values surface in spoken interaction to block justification claims, particularly ultimate-justification claims. Values are claimed to be unconditionally valid as a means of preventing *why* questions. Values thus help in situations of both acute and chronic argumentation failure, at least that's if you believe Niklas Luhmann (1927–1998): "Unlike truths, values are introduced into the communication process not by assertions, which can then be questioned and tested, but by supposition. [...] In other words, values are actualized by allusion and their indisputability consists in this. [...] They make it possible to waive justification. [...] Values are the medium for assuming common ground, which limits what can be said and demanded without determining what should be done."[4]

Values surface in spoken interaction wherever a group wants to distinguish itself from other groups. Communitization through values often aims at the inclusion of everyone, at assembling humanity under one roof. Then, by including some, others are excluded. To preach family values is to exclude single people. Which makes values seem decidedly polemogenous: They want to ostracize, provoke, coerce, to trump other values. Carl

Schmitt, for example, thought that the modern freedom for people to set their own values would inevitably lead "to an eternal battle of values,"[5] thus ushering in a nihilistic global civil war. For him, values aimed at aggressive materialization. In this logic, any value that starts to dominate declares any opposing values to be "unvalues" that must be eliminated. Nevertheless, the logic that values must always produce unvalues seems faulty, given that, after all, values-thinking revolves around hierarchy, ranking. Values are relative to other values; they refer to other values; they're not dependent on unvalues and on the unvaluable. Maybe values are based less on separation than on commonality.

So values surface in spoken interaction to communitize. They are used whenever and wherever it seems advisable to get as many people as possible "on board" with something. One positively ideal place and time for the use of values with integrative intentions is the political speech, delivered on occasions of importance to the state. The values then brought to bear are usually of the greatest possible commonality, so that all those addressed can in some way sign up to them, whatever their specific individual interpretations of them. In Germany, for example, the value of freedom is just as tempting as speechmaking material for representatives of the conservative CDU party as it is to their radical-left counterparts in Die Linke, even if neither is perhaps quite so intoxicated by freedom as their colleagues in the economically liberal FDP or the far-right AfD. If one was to take the word alone at face value, there would seem to be an unshakable values-fellowship under the banner of freedom. Absolutely no one who raises their voice in the contemporary political arena professes to uphold the value of unfreedom—not even the Taliban or North Korean dictators. They just reserve the right to decide what freedom specifically means for them. As one might expect, the freedom upheld by a libertarian member of the supervisory board of a German bank is different from that of a Syrian jihadi who sees freedom flourish only under the shadow of his sword. In each case, the enemies of freedom are always the others—for example, the ones who won't admit that freedom is only possible when the state entirely removes itself from the markets, or the ones who fail to see that only if there is complete equality for all can there be freedom for all, or, finally, the ones whose obdurate hearts are closed to the insight that only the one true faith enables freedom—and that all infidels should therefore die.

Shared values, so frequently invoked, are thus a strange creature with metaphysical quirks. The term suggests that a group of people, or even humanity as a whole, should define itself through common values. With a value like freedom, it seems as if all people can indeed agree on it—and yet this agreement applies only to the one word and not to the thing, which different people clearly understand in totally different ways. Now, we could bracket out the jihadis and the dictators and emphasize that in the Western democracies an agreement on values as more than merely nominal, but as being objectively identical and communally shared, would seem necessary. Once you ignore the extremes, one could say, there's something like a standard distribution of values.

A skeptic would ask whether democracy doesn't in fact consist precisely in the fact that I don't share others' values or that I don't know what kind of values others have—what their preferences are, what they want. And that I then have to come to an arrangement with these others, not because we share common values but because, faced with the possibility that we don't share values while living in a shared space, I must seek terms. Do I not defend my values by leaving others to their own values? A champion of the notion of democratic shared values will counter the skeptical defense with the argument that all of us who consent to participate in the democratic opinion-forming and decision-making process do in fact share values on a second, higher level—for example the values of peace, security, and free expression—values that represent the preconditions for the possibility of particular values that my interlocutor might have but I might not. The skeptic will answer that we might have assumed such second-level values, but they're still not entities in themselves but rather regulative fictions that happen to be useful for our coexistence. I hope that the others share them, but I can't know that. Behind this is the theoretical problem that I can never really discern what kind of values the other has and how they think they have to go about putting these values into practice. The other and their "values orientation" remain, for the time being, opaque to me, and yet I still need to somehow reckon with them. I do this by presupposing a values consensus.

Carl Schmitt blocked out or denied the social cohesion-generating potential of values because he saw the practice of thinking in values categories as an outgrowth of nihilism, which he refused to credit with any positive outcome. Today, by contrast, many of our contemporaries surrender to the sweet hope that it must be possible to unite all people without exception under a single values roof. Both positions are extreme. Often enough we see that "shared values" are proclaimed not in those circumstances in which humanity as a whole is supposed to be taken into account but in circumstances in which the intention is to exclude other humans who aren't supposed to belong to this community. Europeans like to proclaim their own "shared values" when they want to fend off Middle Eastern theocrats or American investors. In doing so, they're propounding not the peaceful coexistence of different, distinct communities with their own values but suggesting that those other communities don't have shared values to speak of at all—*over there* it's a values wasteland. Communities that claim to be based on shared values tend to make themselves absolute and always insist on being right.

Once again, the ironist could interject here. In Germany, she might aver, the only real shared value is the shared value of fear. Even a brief skim through the studies by Walter Krämer (* 1948) is enough to show how often the vocabulary of fear is used in contemporary so-called quality newspapers in Europe. German newspapers are the undefeated champions here—especially the *Süddeutsche Zeitung* and the *Frankfurter Rundschau*—closely followed by the British, while the press in the Latin countries (with the exception of the *Corriere della Sera*) bring up the rear. The conclusion one could draw from this is that the Germans are a herd of frightened deer driven by a panic-mongering media mafia, that the German media is a national disgrace.[6] "The positive man went extinct in the process of evolution. He sat in front of his cave, believed in the saber-toothed tiger's cuteness, and was eaten. Only the misanthropes and paranoiacs survived. Today they work as journalists."[7]

One could also, however, correlate this data with the prosperity and wellbeing of a country: The dominance of fear in the media seems to be most commonly observed in countries that are economically comfortable and politically stable. Might it therefore be reasonable to conclude that fear, administered by the media in regular doses, releases a productive dynamic? Certainly, correlation is no proof of causality, but the idea that fear might have a substantial share in the creation of economic and perhaps also moral values doesn't seem quite so outrageous. The media-fueled fears about deforestation and climate catastrophe, elder poverty and child abuse are significantly intended to change our behavior, to make us better people. No one proclaims fear as their value; in fact, everyone takes as their maxim that they want to overcome or eliminate fear. But if this elimination actually happened, if we unequivocally succeeded in overcoming fear, human life itself might become extinct. So values can also turn up in places and at times in which one doesn't even recognize them as such. The significance of negative values as a precondition for positive values-creation has thus far neither been adequately acknowledged nor become the object of general values discourse.

This values discourse, as it's conducted in practice, often leaves a great deal of vagueness about whether the speaker believes in particular values. It's a kind of speech in which it seems enough to merely assert that one believes in values in general. The shared basis of communication then consists in a common conviction that everything really comes down to values—any values at all. In the fog of this faith in general, unspecified values, the outlines of each concrete value, and thus of each concrete values-conflict, become blurred. Abstract and general values discourse satisfies the conflict-generating nature of values—at least for as long as this values discourse is continued.

So values emerge at diverse places and diverse times in order to fulfill diverse functions—and to reject other functions, for example disambiguation of terminology or precision of observation. But these values aren't things *out there*; rather, they're coinage of varying denomination in processes of verbal understanding and misunderstanding; they can be spent anywhere and at any time. They're multivalent, sometimes even successfully conveying the appearance of omnivalence. If you were to map modern communication, you would find values distributed across the whole landscape, not evenly but accumulated at the periphery and in forgotten corners, because that's where they get left to their own devices.

Those who demand clarity will find it outrageous to think and speak in values, which lack precision, let alone one-to-one correspondence. Which is why self-respecting moral philosophers don't want to know about values—strictly speaking, no one knows anything about them anyway. Nonetheless, values do work somehow, for example in ethics commissions, where they give the impression of a shared ground, even though participants aren't actually standing on a shared ground. If you feed values into one of these commissions or into any other debate on so-called moral questions, you do so in order to shorten the debate, confident in the belief that everyone can come to an agreement even where the differences in the moral-philosophical premises are actually irresoluble. The deontologist and the utilitarian, for example, will never be able to agree on their fundamental assumptions, which in each case they hold to be unambiguous and beyond doubt, but they'll easily be able to agree on the value, the platitude, of freedom. The recourse to values disrupts justification processes. If I feed values into the conversation situation, it's normally because I anticipate agreement—e.g., I won't invoke freedom where a strong tendency of orthodox "Islamist" or "Christianist" adherents believe freedom to be the work of the Devil (the supposed war of the values is a war of morals). Values shut down discourse and put a stop to the endless talking. That's why we need them. Values are abbreviations and thus necessarily polysemous. That too is part of their potential. That's also why they do and should exist.

"Pluralism!" comes a relieved cry from one side and a rueful one from another: This is simply the fate of modernity, in which the living conditions have multiplied and thus the ways in which it's possible to see these living conditions have also multiplied. But what exactly does pluralism mean in relation to values, once you remove the possibility that pluralism might not actually have anything to do with values, because values are in any case inconsequential for acting and living—mere language chimeras to entertain us in our coffee breaks, to help us forget the seriousness of our mortal condition for a few moments? Is pluralism, then, the supposition that everyone may have their own quite personal values according to their taste, regardless of their possible and probable contradiction of the values of others? Or the significantly weaker supposition that everyone merely draws their own individual conclusions from the values that most people, or even the overwhelming majority of people, share, roughly speaking? Is there one particular values framework within which one is only allowed to be plural? It seems safe to presume this, since values that were once widespread, such as inequality between ethnicities or inequality of the sexes, are now stigmatized and penalized in Western societies. Pluralism as values pluralism has clearly stood under rather tight restrictions, despite all appeals to freedom and self-actualization.

Admittedly, these restrictions are subject to change. The *when* and the *where* of values also encompass their evolution—an evolution into which we don't have to read any secret intention of a benevolent nature. They include the question of which values come to the fore under which conditions. Why, for example, has the value of equal opportunity for all people come to the fore in our time? The values genealogist can spare himself any naivete that natural law makes human beings equal and therefore entitled to equal rights—one could just as easily argue from natural law that in our natural state—as experience constantly shows us—we're unequal and therefore entitled to unequal rights. For the business of values genealogy, in order to get to the bottom of when and where which values gained which validity, it's methodologically advisable to separate oneself from one's own ideology and values preferences, at least for a little while. If you want to research the genealogy of values, you should be able to engage and disengage your preferences, to be receptive to other preferences. In the past, scholars proclaimed the scientific ideal of objectivity. Today we can be happy if a researcher takes even the briefest glimpse over the walls of their own ideological garden. Which in turn implies that values pluralism probably doesn't reach all that far.

It's clear, therefore, that values evolution isn't to be understood in a vulgar-Darwinist sense. If we were to take evolution simply as the prevailing of the strongest power interests, that wouldn't explain why in our societies it is the values of consideration to all, by which I mean values of inclusion, equal opportunity, and yes, of "political correctness," that have become so dominant. These are clearly values that can easily run counter to the interests of the majority or of the "ruling class"—for example diminishing their influence or their economic and political capital. The moral-genealogical question here is: Why does the majority nevertheless subject themselves to these values? Because they see in them a promise to increase their own social capital and justify it or expand their legitimization basis, thus offering higher benefits in relation to the costs? Because they can be generous to the disadvantaged from their position of bounty and unchallenged power? Because they're scared of one day being a minority themselves and want to ensure their own protection for this event? Or, by contrast, is this ostentatious submission to values, this devotion to the disadvantaged and weak, merely a cynical gesture, born from the assumption that values are nothing more than linguistic ornamentation, pretty jewels to wear while you ruthlessly pursue your own interests? But perhaps values don't even lie within the scope of our power. Maybe we can't simply engage and disengage them as we choose. "[M]ost of the blocking that shapes our lives works independently of human wishes and intentions."[8] People, like other animals, are blinkered beings. One could argue that values are dispositionally pre-existing "blockers" that pre-form our life (while there are other "blockers" for apes and ants). But some values aren't a priori of the genre: They're not immutable beings existing before all experience. They can change. And even if they are the expression of interests—interests that we plainly have as living (human) beings but that we've never had to or been able to formulate as individual or group-specific interests—we still have the opportunity to place ourselves in a critical relationship with them. Precisely because they are changeable, because they change their *where* and *when*. Because *we* change their *where* and *when*.

Notes

1. Karl Bühler: Sprachtheorie. Die Darstellungsfunktion der Sprache. Mit einem Geleitwort von Friedrich Kainz. Stuttgart/New York 1982, p. 88.
2. Ludger Lütkehaus makes it hauntingly clear just how much effort is associated with capturing non-speaking, silence, in art: Stille. Schweigen. Musik. Marburg an der Lahn 2015, p. 20: "'White painting', like John Cage's composition of silence, his music of non-music, is, however, the paradoxically logical way of not *saying* anything and precisely because of that to say *nothing*."
3. Evidence of the latter was shown by Volker Heeschen for villages among the Eipo and Yalenang in Papua in: Hütte, Weiler oder sakrale Mitte? Über Dörfer im Bergland von Papua. In: Philip Ajouri/Wolfert von Rahden/Andreas Urs Sommer (eds.): Das Dorf = Zeitschrift für Ideengeschichte, no. IX/2. Munich 2015, pp. 19–28, here p. 26–28
4. Niklas Luhmann: Die Gesellschaft der Gesellschaft. Frankfurt a. M. 1997, Bd. 1, S. 343.
5. Carl Schmitt: Die Tyrannei der Werte. In: Eberhard Jüngel/Sepp Schelz/Carl Schmitt: Die Tyrannei der Werte.. Hamburg 1979, pp. 11–43, here p. 31.
6. Walter Krämer: Ein Volk von Panikmachern. Über Risikoverzerrung und Verfügbarkeitsheuristik. In: Forschung & Lehre 9/2015, pp. 714–715, here p. 715.
7. Dieter Nuhr: Das Geheimnis des perfekten Tages. Cologne 2015, p. 75.
8. Paul Feyerabend: The Conquest of Abundance: A Tale of Abstraction versus the Richness of Being ed. Bert Terpstra, Chicago and London 1999, p. 27.

CHAPTER 6

Excursus I: Values and Human Rights

Abstract This chapter, "Values and Human Rights," explores the complex interplay between human rights, values, and societal dynamics within the European context. While the European Human Rights Convention and the EU Charter of Fundamental Rights mention values, their relationship remains elusive. The chapter delves into the vagueness of "common values" and their connection to peace and examines the tensions between universality, individual rights, and societal contexts. The evolution of human rights reveals a shift from freedom-based rights towards equality-oriented claims. The chapter scrutinizes the dual nature of human rights, serving as protections against harm and as expressions of demands for societal standards. It highlights the challenges of justifying human rights, especially amid shifting social paradigms, and the potential for values discourse to provide a flexible foundation for their functional stabilization. Ultimately, the chapter underscores the intricate and evolving nature of human rights and their dependence on ongoing societal negotiations.

This excursus is based on a lecture that I delivered under the title "Using/needing human rights. On the philosophical relevance of their historicity" at the Colloquium Rauricum on August 28, 2015, at Castelen/Augst. A complete version is due to appear in 2016 in the book of the Colloquia Raurica conference proceedings on human rights edited by Kurt Seelmann.

A. U. Sommer, *Values*,
https://doi.org/10.1007/978-3-031-42159-4_6

Keywords Values • Human rights • European Union • Universality • Freedom • Equality • Social dynamics • Justification • Normative fallacy • Underdetermination

While the European Human Rights Convention of 1950 has nothing to say about values, the Preamble to the European Union Charter of Fundamental Rights of 2000 mentions them three times. The very first sentence reads: "The peoples of Europe, in creating an ever closer union among them, are resolved to share a peaceful future based on common values."[1] The formulation remains vague about how exactly these "common values" relate to the resolution by said peoples to enjoy a "peaceful future," while the reassuring expression "on the basis of" draws a veil over the nature of the relationship between these values and the resolute pursuit of future peace. Are the values the efficient causes of this resolution or perhaps the final causes? Are they the conditions of possibility or merely rhetorical flourishes? Further guidance comes in the second sentence: "Conscious of its spiritual and moral heritage, the Union is founded on the indivisible, universal values of human dignity, freedom, equality and solidarity."[2] These four concrete values are propagated as indivisible and universal, a claim that goes beyond the European framework, but a legal text can hardly be expected to substantiate these values or concern itself with whether they can be harmonized with each other. Whoever has taken it upon themselves to speak in the name of the "peoples of Europe" seems to be untroubled that human dignity remains vague, and that freedom, equality, and solidarity can easily clash with each other. The question of the relationship between these values and the fundamental rights that are supposed to be the real subject of the Charter is still moot on the third mention: "The Union contributes to the preservation and to the development of these common values while respecting the diversity of the cultures and traditions of the peoples of Europe as well as the national identities of the Member States and the organization of their public authorities at national, regional and local levels."[3] That these values are to be preserved is unsurprising, but it seems a little odd that they can somehow be *developed*. Is this supposed to mean that they're not quite so solid and unchanging as one might have supposed from the claim of their indivisibility and universality? That they are after all subject to the vagaries of time, that they have come to be via historical processes and are historically transient? Or is the mention of "development" supposed to mean simply that while they have not yet been realized everywhere, the intention is to realize them everywhere in future?

The European legislature must be at a loss for explaining and justifying its ideas if it has to seek refuge in such ontologically obscure entities as "values," claiming firstly their universality and indivisibility, secondly their mutual compatibility (which seems controversial, at least in the case of freedom and equality), as well as, thirdly, leaving open the question of how the values should be related to the fundamental rights (what does "based on" mean?). When it comes to the third point, one can nevertheless note that the concretely named four values of human rights, freedom, equality, and solidarity comprise the titles of the first four chapters of the Charter, in which the relevant fundamental rights are listed—albeit the singular "freedom" is divided up into a telling plurality of "freedoms." According to the text-logic of the Charter, values are thus a kind of totalizing umbrella term or genus name for a series of individual fundamental rights. Might they then at the same time perform a *justifying* function for fundamental rights? Indeed, in the case of human dignity, it's explicitly claimed that this is at the same time a value and, according to Article 1, the first fundamental right. Should fundamental or human rights be considered values in order that they can be conserved in a sphere of untouchability? "The fixing of such themes as fundamental rights in the constitution removes them from discussion, however much they may also remain the object of deferential interpretation. Their dogmatic treatment as untouchable values reinforces this taboo and gives them a moral consecration."[4]

The European legislature finds itself in a quandary when it comes to determining the foundations of positive law. It doesn't want to appear as a positive lawmaking instance, so it suggests that the fundamental human rights in some way transcendentally precede the rule of law. Nevertheless, to anyone even slightly informed, it's clear that fundamental and human rights are subject to a process of historical becoming—that for most of its history, humanity had neither the term "human rights" nor the things to which it refers. The supposed universality and noncontingency of fundamental and human rights are not a historical universality and noncontingency but an *ought*. Not even an avowed human rights universalist would claim that human rights have always applied, like the three laws of thermodynamics, rather being discovered over the course of history.

Underlying the concept of human rights is a different conception of the human than the one that dominated for the majority of human history, which wasn't necessarily an ignorant or essentially faulty conception. For Aristotle, for example, it was a matter of course that there was the "natural slave," who belonged to another person and who only participated in reason, in *logos*, if he did so through another person.[5] If there are natural free men or natural slaves, then it is prohibited to think of equally attributing them something like human rights, at least those listed under main headings in the *Charter of Human Rights:* Human Dignity, Freedom, Equality, and Solidarity. Now, it's easy to say that the Aristotelian idea of humanity is simply unenlightened and antiquated; it's notably harder to justify how this idea of humanity is untrue or false in the way that we would now claim for large swathes of Aristotelian physics. The anthropology of pre-modern philosophy is simply a different one from the one that predominates in the contemporary world and that forms the basis of the human rights concept. If you want to provide enlightenment about human rights, you have to at least reach an understanding about the underlying concept of the human.

And here you bump into a remarkable finding, though one that is overlooked in the debate about human rights. Over the course of modernity, human beings have successively been stripped of their metaphysical and religious attributes. They are no longer believed to be the image of God; they lose their privileges as the crown of Creation. Even for radical thinkers of the Enlightenment, the novelty had already worn off the notion that human beings might not be different from an animal or a machine[6]—a thought that found widespread resonance in the nineteenth century. In the theory of evolution, humans were understood as the product of a general zoological process of development in which the human being wasn't some kind of end goal. Humans are relegated to being just another animal among animals[7]; they lose their exceptional status in the structure of lifeforms. The development of modern anthropology presents itself as the process of a radical humbling.

What's surprising is that this radical humbling, this metaphysical depotentialization of the human, goes hand-in-hand with a fundamental upgrading of the human in terms of law and, yes, human rights, an upgrading that applies to every single human, entirely independently of their status, gender, income, or actions. The more that metaphysical contamination of concepts of the human fell away, and the more that humans were relegated to an animal existence among animals, the more resolutely the forces that shaped mentality, up to and including national and supranational legislators, proved willing to ascribe the human being a new metaphysical dignity by means of human rights. Gradually, the person was sacralized.[8]

From this perspective, therefore, human rights do not seem to be the result of a deepened, enhanced insight into what actually makes a person, based on the discovery of the true nature of the human. Rather, human rights are shown to be the result of human history, a history in which the radical self-humbling of the human is confronted with something else: the concept of inalienable human dignity, freedom, equality. One could say that human rights were created to make it bearable to confront the scientifically based insight that the human is an animal among animals. To make it possible to forget this insight.

The emergence of human rights is based on traditional, albeit modified, notions of natural law. Admittedly, nothing normative follows from this, because these notions of natural law are hard to bring into the present. An approach that's just as full of pitfalls is the attempt, originating from discourse ethics, to retroactively legitimize human rights. If you postulate a discourse free of domination, an ideally a priori communication community in which all discourse-participants must agree that the most reasonable and best thing is to grant all affected parties the same rights, you enter into a vicious circle. The concept of the domination-free discourse itself presupposes that which in fact still needs to be proved: Namely, that all discourse-participants are in principle equal. In discourse ethics, therefore, the justification for human rights takes the human rights-based commandment of equal opportunities as its unevidenced premise. If you don't share this premise, you won't be satisfied with the justification, which obscures the specific discourse participants by emphasizing solely the arguments that require assent, the arguments whose power no reasonable being could escape. For the critic of discourse ethics there are, in questions of praxis (in contrast to mathematics or logic) no neutral and compelling arguments beyond the persons who make them. And what if these persons are not equal but unequal?

What should the normative justification of a historic and thus contingent phenomenon like human rights actually be good for? In all the attempts to make such a justification, a normative fallacy easily emerges. This fallacy consists in giving in to a social pressure, perceived as normative, and claiming undeniable truth for a hypothesis for which there are no extra-normative empirical findings, or even one that contradicts these findings. The normativist fallacy consists of deriving from the (societally) dominant assumption that something is noncontingently true that it really is noncontingently and necessarily true.

Perhaps more can be won from the reality of human rights for their legitimation than from attempts to construct an ultimate justification. Certainly, these legitimization approaches would be only provisional—but anything beyond that might be unavailable under earthly conditions with earthly objects. Human rights can also be used differently in different contexts. Three examples, taken as symptoms:

In June 2015, the Greek Supreme Court, in agreement with the Greek parliamentary president, ruled that the spending cuts demanded by the "institutions"(of the EU) and the costs of debt services were in breach of human rights. Specifically, the court found, the pension cuts already implemented by the contracts for the first rescue packet were injurious to human rights because they made it impossible for many pensioners to enjoy a decent standard of life. Human rights are thus no longer understood as negative claims by the individual against a state that is to leave them as far as possible in peace. They have become positive claims. I can demand of my state that it provides for me when I'm not able to do so myself. And if this state cannot fulfill such guarantees, for example because it's bankrupt, I can transfer this claim to a supranational level—for example the European Union, which has to take responsibility for my needs. In this understanding, the community has a comprehensive duty of care for the individual, who has no comparable duty to care for the community. And this imbalance could lead to the inner erosion of the community. Not so provisional conclusion: Solidarity is something that the individual can demand from the other—specifically from the state and supranational institutions. The scope of these demands is expanding rapidly. 2. Freedom of expression, as one of the fundamental human rights, is at least nominally highly valued. After the attack on *Charlie Hebdo*, hundreds of thousands of people made a seemingly brave profession of solidarity with the words "Je suis Charlie." Some of these people, however, were those who otherwise call for legal penalization of undesirable statements against, for example, Islam, immigrants, or gay people. In France, there are laws against defamation, some of which are subject to draconian penalties, even for notably general statements, for example purely general doubts that Islam is compatible with Enlightenment European civilization.[9] The vehement defenders of freedom of expression see dark times coming for the Western world, with this freedom being suppressed on the basis of "political correctness," imagining a conspiracy at work with the goal of making all people equal.

If you take a broader view than day-to-day political squabbling, however, you'll make a more cautious prediction. Certainly, John Stuart Mill's (1806–1873) view that everyone must always be able to say anything, no matter how absurd, is deserving of great honor: "diversity [is] not an evil, but a good."[10] But this view emerged from the world of British gentlemen's clubs rather than the modern digital mass society in which every opinion of every person can be heard at any time and in any place. Where freedom of expression is restricted today, it's significantly the result of fear of offense. If someone perceives verbal utterances aimed not against individual persons but against general concepts, such as a worldview or a sexual orientation, as offenses, then that is connected to a general lowering of the threshold of sensitivity and pain that is characteristic of modernity. Europeans perceive offense and pain in experiences that our ancestors would simply have put up with. On the other hand, many people who migrate to Europe, especially Muslims, perceive insults to their religion as a fundamental attack on themselves. This isn't the sinking of the individual sensitivity threshold but the rise to dominance of the pre-modern idea that opinions, in and of themselves, have a destructive, magical power—an idea that should really flatter every "opinion-maker." Not so provisional conclusion: Freedom of expression meets its limits as soon as the constantly sinking sensitivity and pain threshold of potential recipients is reached. As a human right, it's only safe from harm if the expressed opinion is certain not to upset anyone. If the opinion is completely neutral.

It's revealing to see how all manner of groups go to great efforts to place their interests under the protection of human rights. Some of these groups are populations who invoke what has become known as the third generation of human rights to claim their right of self-determination against a state in which they feel insufficiently represented or even oppressed. Others are social minorities who claim rights that have allegedly hitherto been reserved for the majority. For example, the demand that the right to marriage must apply to everyone regardless of their sexual orientation. All these endeavors aim for inclusion: Everyone should be able to have everything. General equalization seems to be the consequence. And then there's the other, complementary side: In the event that one cannot successfully assert one's group interests with recourse to the general and universal human rights, one can simply devise one's own catalog of human rights that serves these interests. One example of this is the Cairo Declaration on Human Rights in Islam of 1990, which proclaims Sharia as the basis of an appropriate understanding of human rights. Not so provisional conclusion: The expansion of human rights claims raises the question of the limits to their growth. Human rights seem to be justified by their general utility only insofar as they don't get completely captured by particular causes. This danger is built into the structure of human rights, the danger that they become entitlements of persons and groups of people. One might think that these claims, precisely because they are positive claims, can be indefinitely escalated. Ultimately it seems as if equalization and particularization often go hand-in-hand, however much they do battle against each other in the arena of politics and media.

If we take these three usage examples as symptoms, the first thing we discern is a shift to the social human rights. In fact, most Europeans are now human rights beneficiaries, but the development is moving away from the freedom rights to the equality rights. The unresolved tension between equality and freedom in the traditional human rights catalogs is shifting ever farther towards equality—which reduces the tension, but also the freedom. What Tacitus ruefully identified as *libido servitii,* the "desire for slavery,"[11] takes on a quite new sound in the modern world.

Today one might tend towards lamenting the general equalization and social-democratization. However, this development is nothing more than an answer to the vast expansion of the scope of freedom in modernity, which has opened up previously undreamed-of possibilities for the individual. It seems as if contemporary human rights politics, as a politics of inclusion, wants to contain the limitless expansion—especially the economic expansion—of these scopes of freedom.

The modern age is characterized not only by the extension of the individual's scope of choice but also by the development of abstract, supra individual institutions and a powerful wave of differentiation between diverse societal subsystems. This puts the individual into highly varied functional contexts; highly varied role requirements are placed upon the individual, who in pre-modernity usually only had a limited repertoire of roles. Human rights form, as it were, the lowest common denominator for each of these diverse roles of the modern individual. They thus make an essential contribution to the smooth running of the social machinery. The disillusioning anthropological insight at the threshold to modernity, that the human is an animal among animals, is clearly not able to meet the demands of the modern human's highly diverse roles in highly complex societies. This therefore creates the impression that the modern person is an entity entitled to a value in itself. This might be a contra-factual postulate—but it's an extremely helpful one for societies in which people credit themselves with capability for so many different kinds of tasks. Human societies aren't termite nests. If you grant people all the rights—if you treat them as if they have these rights innately, along with an immortal soul—you can get the best out of them.

Theoretically, the dilemma is unresolvable. On the one hand, we assume that the value of an individual person is absolute, that nothing can cancel it out, that human dignity is untouchable. On the other, every person experiences themselves as limited, fallible, fragile; in brief, as incomplete, relative—as a mortal animal among other mortal animals. Practically, by contrast, we know very well how to deal with this dilemma. The more unstable the normative basis of human rights, the more excessive and extensive they become in number and in demand: a strategy of drowning-out, of covering up the instability of the normative basis with a plethora of codifications. An alternative explanation is that this is a strategy of functional stabilization. It's precisely because the ground is unsteady that one constructs the building as big as possible and, above all, in such a way that everyone thinks it's fit for its purpose.

Human rights serve, firstly, to protect humans from themselves and their peers. Secondly, they articulate humans' demands of themselves and of their peers. There's no longer a traditional social hierarchy or natural order that could protect people and to which they could address claims for what they are owed.

In relation to human rights and to the values that supposedly underlie them, underdetermination is neither regrettable nor pernicious. In fact, it's desirable. We don't know specifically what our interlocutor's values are, even when we're discussing values with them. We always talk about values as if we do know. It's not only the underdetermined nature of the term "value" that's a decisive advantage of values discourse but also the underdetermined nature of its concretization. An ironist would say that transcendental philosophy has thus found its way into everyday moral discourse, because when we talk about values we are, as it were, talking about the conditions of the possibility of good action, about "value orientation," rather than about the concrete good itself, and we assume that the other person, who after all must also be "values-guided," certainly also wants the best …

With this kind of basis in values, human rights seem to rest on thin ice. One can derive more or less anything from values, especially if one refrains from explication. But this results in manifold functionalizability. Perhaps human rights owe their underdetermination first to their extensive usability.

Notes

1. Charter of Fundamental Rights of the European Union. The Member States https://eur-lex.europa.eu/legal-content/EN/ALL/?uri=CELEX:12012P/TXT
2. ibid.
3. ibid., p. 41.
4. Niklas Luhmann: Grundrechte als Institution. Ein Beitrag zur politischen Soziologie. Berlin 1965, p. 8.
5. Aristotle: Politics 1254a.
6. See Julien Offray de La Mettrie: Œuvres philosophiques. Nouvelle édition, corrigée & augmentée. Berlin 1774, vol. 1, p. 347 f.
7. See Andreas Urs Sommer: Kommentar zu Nietzsches Der Antichrist. Ecce homo. Dionysos- Dithyramben. Nietzsche contra Wagner = Historischer und kritischer Kommentar zu Friedrich Nietzsches Werken. Ed. Heidelberger Akademie der Wissenschaften. Vol. g/2. Berlin/Boston 2013, p. 83 f.
8. Cf. in the further development of the approached of Émile Durkheim, particularly Hans Joas: Die Sakralität der Person. Eine neue Genealogie der Menschenrechte. Berlin 2011.
9. See Jonathan Turley: Charlies falsche Freunde. In: Schweizer Monat. Die Autorenzeitschrift für Politik, Wirtschaft und Kultur, no. 1023, February 2015, pp. 12–15.
10. John Stuart Mill: On Liberty/Über die Freiheit. Deutsch – englisch. Übersetzung von Bruno Lemke. Mit Anhang und Nachwort ed. Bernd Gräfrath. Stuttgart 2009, p. 160.
11. Publius Cornelius Tacitus: Historien I 90, 3.

CHAPTER 7

The Unstable Recovery Position. How Is a Value Positioned?

Abstract In this chapter, titled "The Unstable Recovery Position: How is a Value Positioned?", the discussion revolves around the concept of values and their positioning within the framework of human communication. The chapter explores the distinction between the "where" of a value and its position or situation. Values are likened to entities that exist in various locations but are not necessarily pinned down in specific positions. The chapter delves into the challenges of understanding the existence of values, touching on debates about moral objectivity and linguistic analysis. The relationship between values and clarity is questioned, and the notion of values as cosmopolitan entities is examined. The tension between the absoluteness claim of values and their relational nature is explored, using historical and philosophical perspectives. The chapter critiques the idea of an absolute set of values dominating historical progress and raises concerns about the potential saturation of values leading to diminishing utility. Ultimately, the chapter invites readers to consider the nuanced and complex nature of values and their placement in the tapestry of human discourse.

Keywords Value positioning • Where vs. position • Cosmopolitan values • Absoluteness of values • Normative projects • Values saturation • Marginal utility of values • Communication pluriverse • Human communication

A. U. Sommer, *Values*,
https://doi.org/10.1007/978-3-031-42159-4_7

How does the question of the *where* of a value differ from the question of its position, its situation? To the question "where?", the answer might be, for example, "it's in the lyceum" on "it's in the agora"; to the question "in what position?", by contrast, "it's sitting" or "it's lying".[1] If one were to cartograph modern communication, one could name countless locations where values can be found—scattered across the whole field of human speaking—but this would not be the same as pinning down their positions in all these locations. It could be that the values in these locations lead downtrodden communicative existences in the shadow of dominant forces, defiled and robbed of all their power. But it could be that they not only hold their ground in these locations, upright and proud, but are also in charge of what happens there. Finally, and in fact probably, it might be that they're located in different positions in different locations. It might be that one value is a backbencher in the parliament of our decision-making and the other is a tyrant who brooks no dissent, that one value plays the head chef in our psychological household, another the house slave or lodger, while yet another boldly declares itself the head of the family. Values might not be omnivalent, but they are multivalent, depending on how and where they appear—and they're also polytopic: They can be used anywhere, and they can find their way in everywhere.

But we're still only talking here about the diverse locations and positions of values within the structure of human communication. We haven't even begun to talk about whether these values actually exist! John Leslie Mackie (1917–1981) once conceded that the normal moral judgment of everyday language claims objectivity. This judgment, he continued, presupposes that there are objective values that are not merely the product of human communication: "the traditional moral concepts of the ordinary man as well as of the main line of western philosophers are concepts of objective value."[2] For that reason, mere linguistic analysis does not suffice for metaethical reflection; we've made a basic error if we indulge in this values-realistic suggestion. For Mackie, the assumption of moral objectivity implicit in our moral speaking is nothing more than a false doctrine.[3]

To use it is to return to the brusque either-or of being and not-being. In this logic, being wouldn't even *be* being, at least not a serious being, if it were in communication. Physical objects would have being—as, perhaps, would mental objects that can be clearly and distinctly grasped—such as numbers. Values, by contrast, can't be spotted like a skein of geese in the evening sky or chiseled out like a granite block in a quarry, nor do they result from one-to-one mental operations, as the number four does from the addition of one and three or the division of eight by two. Admittedly, those who attribute existence to objects that are derived from logical reasoning but not from observation—the number four can't be observed; at most you could observe four hornets or four crocuses—are on unsteady ground. To them, the difference between mental objects like numbers and mental objects like values would chiefly be that the former can be clearly and unambiguously defined while the latter can't. The ambiguousness or unambiguousness of the definition would then be the defining existence criterion. The diffuse, conceptually blurry being of values would have to serve as proof of their actual non-being—that's if they even have a conceptual rather than purely emotional being in the first place. In this either-or, the values scurrilously refuse to stick to the maxim that "[w]hat can be said at all can be said clearly."[4] If Wittgenstein is right, they can't be said at all, and don't even cut it as potential mental objects with *aspirations* toward being. But why should, of all things, *being* be exclusively allocated to the realm of the clearly thought, while the unclear sinks into non-being? The vagueness or blurriness of a thing is in no way proof of its non-existence. We don't know if values are blurry in themselves or are merely perceived by us as blurry and thought of unclearly. We won't question the existence of the skein of geese or the granite block just because at night we see them only dimly. We won't question the existence of love just because we can't formulate a clear concept of it. We see some things more distinctly, some less distinctly. We think some things more clearly, some less clearly. That has nothing to do with their being or non-being.

And—as I've already said—there are gradations of existing. Why shouldn't communicative being also be such a gradation? Very many things, apart from values, principally exist in this way. Blurred existence increases the need for communication. If something seems unclear and indistinct, it needs to be clarified in speech and counter-speech. I experience values not directly but through the circumstance that they are brokered to me communicatively—whether verbally or nonverbally ("a slap on the wrist never did anyone any harm"). That's what eager education bureaucrats call "values education" and put into the curriculum—despite not having a more distinct understanding or a clearer concept of what values are than anyone else. The crucial thing is that we talk about values and get the students to talk about them too.

In order to gain a little more clarity and distinctness about the essential communicative being of values, one should expand the question horizon beyond the *where* and *when*. If the assumptions about the *where* and *when* concretize—specifically, if they've concretized in human communication whenever a need surfaces for such things as justification, interpretation, and motivation—one will want to know in which position each of these values finds itself. What is their place in life?

Values, as Niklas Grouls has observed, are first and foremost cosmopolitan in the communications pluriverse. That's why they also share the handicap of other citizens of the world—never being able to establish themselves as natives with a right to have a say. Cosmopolitans are suspected of being constantly on the point of leaving, not prepared to put their heart and soul into participating in local life. The position of values, when thus seen as cosmopolitans, seems evasive and lacking in power. A reputation of nomadism and thus of commitment phobia is associated with cosmopolitan values. As soon as you want to rely on them, they tend to have already disappeared or be hiding behind a mountain of "practical constraints."

Moral utility values quickly forfeit their cosmopolitan luster once they're put to use. Then they suddenly become site-specific, no matter how big the particular word chosen to describe them may seem. When a Bavarian politician from the conservative CSU party speaks of family values, he means something different than when a Swedish Social Democrat discusses the same topic. In addition to their drive for cosmopolitanism, a contradictory tendency towards self-regionalization and sedimentation inheres to values.

Existing in a state of tension with this nomadization of values is the absoluteness claim that often accompanies them, as discussed above in the chapter on connecting and relativizing. Related to position and location, absoluteness would mean that the values are compulsory, for everyone, regardless of situation and perspective. In a lecture on ethics given in 1929 or 1930, Ludwig Wittgenstein (1889–1951) distinguished between relative and absolute value judgments. Relative value judgments, he said, are really only a particular form of fact claims. His example: 'Instead of saying "This is the right way to Grantchester," I could equally well have said, "This is the right way you have to go if you want to get to Grantchester in the shortest time".'[5] An absolute value judgment, by contrast, would require that whatever was judged of unqualified value must be considered so in every respect and for everyone without exception. The absolute right way would be the way that absolutely everyone should go under all circumstances. The absolute good or the absolute value would be something that everyone, regardless of their tendencies and preferences, would have to strive to bring forth or feel guilty for not striving to bring forth.[6] While Wittgenstein considers it a chimera to claim that a set of circumstances like this is scientifically true[7] and thus holds that ethics is something that can't be science, at the same time he pays his deep respect to the tendency of the human intellect to formulate such absolute value judgments. He repudiates any attempt to mock this tendency.[8]

We, however, *pace* Wittgenstein, don't have to share this respect. We can take the dubious tendency to formulate absolute value judgments not necessarily as a general trademark of the human spirit but quite coolly as a pathology of the judgment-making capacity that appears only under quite particular historical conditions—under an absolutist monotheistic regime during the phases of its inexorable demise, for example, when God has been liquidated but the moral attitude that's based on Him remains.

Assuming the absoluteness of values (or of one value) for a moment, what would it mean for each location and position? Quite clearly, not only that each of these values would be in an entirely specific position. After all, a specific position, a specific location would mean that the values in question were not in fact absolute, because they would not be in a whole range of other positions and locations. If you wanted to believe in the absoluteness of values, you would also have to claim not just that they have an obligating force that guards them from any relativization by other values and by non-values (for example interests, preferences, physical objects). The card-carrying values ontologist would additionally claim that they were in every conceivable position. The values would have to lie and sit, stand and fall, hold fast and let go—all at the same time. Values placed absolutely would have to occupy all positions at the same time. They would be entirely miraculous entities that no one could get a clear picture or perspective of because they would be not only everywhere but everywhere in every possible position. Such an idea roughly corresponds to the level of reflection of the very first philosophical testimonies that are preserved from Ancient Greece, in which it is reported that Thales of Miletus (c. 624–547 BCE) claimed everything was full of gods.[9] If it seems to you to be going too far to conclude from this that everything is full of values, and that absolute values must exist in absolutely every position, you'd be curtailing the absoluteness of values. They would then be at best relatively absolute—whatever that would mean.

If the archaicizing hypothesis that values are position-absolute seems unworkable, the alternative hypothesis, that values could in principle exist in all possible positions, but not in all of them at the same time, seems more reasonable. Equally plausible is the additional assumption that whichever position values are in, they're always together with other values and with non-values. They never stand, sit, or move for themselves alone. Part of the position of values involves being in relationship with other things, with other values. No value can stand for itself—or without someone for whom it is a value. Values are thus in a "with-world position."

Some people are doing good business with values in the "with-world position." The historian Heinrich August Winkler (b. 1938), for example, sees the "history of the West" as a history in which values take on a dominating attitude towards non-values—for example towards conditions of economic existence. And this history presents itself to him, moreover, as one in which particular values gradually prevail and overcome countervalues. For Winkler, "the West" is pursuing a "normative project," of realizing the "values that developed under historically unique conditions over centuries in a part of Europe, the 'Latin' part of the old continent, shaped by the Western Church, and found their classical expression in the American and French human rights declarations of the late eighteenth century. The transatlantic West thus had the theme that it would have to work away at from then on."[10] Human rights, equality, and general democratization: For the values-loving historian, these are defining aspects of Western and universal history.

Winkler's history of the West is a modern edition of the speculative-universalist philosophy of history developed in the eighteenth century.[11] Like its venerable predecessor, Winkler's history is intended above all to offer reassurance and comfort. In this history, values are on the one hand the historical subjects themselves; on the other they are a "project" and as such drawn on by a somewhat ominous historical subject called "the West." It's a secular salvation story, characterized by ideas and values conflicts, but all manner of mishaps may occur along the way—the stricken values end up lying on their side in a precarious recovery position in the gutter, covered in bandages and a painterly spattering of blood—but the long trek into the light is unstoppable. No time is wasted on the thought that "cultural circles" aren't acting persons and cannot therefore pursue "normative projects." Should it not occur to any historian, at least one not angling for a job as official historian to the Berlin court, that this strange conglomeration "the West," perhaps in contrast to other "cultural circles," is distinguished precisely by its failure to have formed a single, homogenous values set, a unified worldview? Has there not been a positive abundance of "normative projects" hatched in "the West"—including ones that distinguish in principle between the faithful and infidels (and thus, in contrast to Winkler's arguments for the supposed equalizing effect of Christianity, make this distinction into a criterion for deciding on life and death)? Or ones that take up arms against the supposedly inherently Western striving for equality and human rights, believing that equality is by nature not unjust but just, since human beings are fundamentally different from each other, such that each deserves not the same but only what is rightfully due to him?

Even assuming that Winkler has reconstructed the "normative project" of "the West" with historical accuracy, how does he manage, as a historian, to derive some kind of desired state from this mere statement of (supposed) historical fact? Why does he completely blank out the contingency from which this Western normative project is no exception, when the eternal task of the historian consists precisely in contingency? Should we not be able to demand of a historian that, when reconstructing a "normative project," for example that of Confucianism or of the Māori, they should describe what it consists of, simply and *sine ira et studio*—instead of lecturing us on our continuing duty to uphold it?[12] Might it not be better to leave this kind of task to the preachers? No, and again no, is the unmistakable answer to the two last questions—not if a scholar wants to pander to the current sensibilities of politicians who like to see themselves as the vanguard of historical progress. But maybe their claim of "defending shared Western values" is nothing more than the continuation of the old imperialist demand for global authority via other means.

But either way: Winkler's *History of the West* offers, firstly, a wonderful example of how to write counterfactual history. How would things be if (almost) everything consisted of nothing more than values and their conflicts? Secondly, it's a wonderful example of how to bring values into compromising situations—an example of the fatal situation in which values can in practice end up in everyday communication today. Values are easily overwhelmed, being delicate, ethereal creatures, in some cases short-lived ones—even if Winkler attributes them a long genealogy.

Much is demanded of values—they're supposed to be able to do everything, even in the position of subjects with world-historical agency. On the other hand, in the logic of Winkler's story, they're under acute threat. History—at least the more recent history of the "West"—appears as a process of concentration: A jumbled diversity of values gives way to the dominance of a smaller set of values that answer to shouts of "Western!", "free!", or "democratic!". If certain values advance in this story into a position of dominance, or even hegemony, it's at the cost of other values that they push out of the way. The pattern of this secular salvation story is thus one of displacement, of the usurpation of habitat. Instead of looming values inflation, the threat for us of the gradual and far from smooth rise to dominance of Western values is a rising scarcity of values, brought about by elimination of competing values. And that puts these few remaining values into a particular position—that of no longer being oppressed, inferior, languishing injured on the roadside of development, but of becoming dominant and having the final say on action and life. As a history of values empowerment, Winkler's secular values salvation story perfectly serves that part of the *Zeitgeist* that is the contemporary demand for illusion. The values—by which he means particular "Western" values—gradually become as close as conceivably possible to the archaicizing hypothesis of the position-absoluteness of values. The only difference is that the values in this version only become absolute over history—they weren't always absolute. Thanks to a Hegel infection, we get beyond Thales.

Assuming for a moment that history really is taking this inevitable course, and we can therefore look forward to the undisputed dominance of Western values, we'd still quickly be faced by the question of declining marginal utility. The more widely that scarce goods become available, the more their utility declines and satiety sets in. We eat one piece of cake with pleasure, and maybe a second and third too, but by the sixth or eighth piece, even the most voracious of us will reach marginal utility, and the tenth piece is good for nothing but nausea. Is the economic theory of marginal utility also relevant for moral values? If we have too many values, or values in every position, might that not lead to values-need-satiety, which could easily veer into values-disgust? In the case of the value of freedom, for example, could that not easily exceed its marginal utility?

Values draw strength from their scarcity—from the suggestion that they're scarce. That's why it's not necessarily desirable to have them in every possible location and position. Why not leave them imperfectly balanced on their side in the recovery position?

Notes

1. See Aristotle: Kategorien 2a 1–2 (Aristotle: Categoriae et Liber de Interpretatione. Recognovit brevique adnotatione critica instruxit L. Minio-Paluello. Oxford 1961, p. 5).

2. John Leslie Mackie: Ethics. Inventing Right and Wrong. London 1990, p. 35.
3. Ibid., p. 49.
4. Ludwig Wittgenstein: Tractatus logico-philosophicus. Frankfurt a. M. 1960, sentence 4.116.
5. Ludwig Wittgenstein: A Lecture on Ethics. In: The Philosophical Review, vol. 74, no. 1, January 1965, pp. 3–12, here p. 6.
6. Ibid., p. 7.
7. ibid.
8. Ibid., p. 12.
9. Aristotle: De anima 411a 8–9 (Hermann Diels/Walther Kranz [eds.]: Die Fragmente der Vorsokratiker. 5. Aufl. Berlin 1951, Fragment 11 A 22).
10. Heinrich August Winkler: Geschichte des Westens. Vol. 4: Die Zeit der Gegenwart. Munich 2015, p. 12.
11. See the more comprehensive treatment of this in Andreas Urs Sommer: Sinnstiftung durch Geschichte? Zur Entstehung spekulativuniversalistischer Geschichtsphilosophie zwischen Bayle und Kant. Basel 2006.
12. A propos projects: one should remember what David Hume recommended at the end of his essay Against Projects – namely, to throw them into the fire (Andreas Urs Sommer: Lexikon der imaginären philosophischen Werke. Berlin 2012, p. 258).

CHAPTER 8

Miracles of Motivation and Guarantors of Paralysis. What Do Values Have? What Do They Do?

Abstract This chapter, titled "Miracles of Motivation and Guarantors of Paralysis: What Do Values Have? What Do They Do?" delves into the intricate nature of values and their role in shaping human behavior. The chapter challenges the idea that values are merely abstract concepts that shape individuals in a deterministic manner. It explores contrasting viewpoints from the political and sociological perspectives, highlighting the tension between values as motivators and values as impotent forces. The chapter examines how values can both motivate and paralyze action, with emphasis on the complex interplay between values, actions, and emotions. It contemplates whether values derive their motivating power from lack or surplus, and whether they function as self-verification mechanisms or triggers for guilt. The discourse delves into the intertwined relationships between values, conscience, debt, and modern morality, ultimately questioning the impact of values on individual and societal dynamics in a world of evolving economic and moral landscapes.

Keywords Motivation • Paralysis • Conscience • Sociological perspective • Political perspective • Moral emotions • Debt economy • Self-verification • Guilt

A. U. Sommer, *Values*,
https://doi.org/10.1007/978-3-031-42159-4_8

The political profession never tires of telling us: Values shape us, they make us who we are. Well, they certainly should do. If they didn't, they'd be meaningless.

To take these fine-sounding words at face value, however, might send you down a dangerous path. After all, surely this would make people simply a moldable mass, a product, a function of their values? If it were true, we wouldn't choose values; we'd be chosen by them as their obedient stooges. It would, for example, be impossible today to remove oneself from the values of freedom, peace, and health; to avoid being shaped by them. Is that what the politicians are gently trying to communicate to us?

The sociological profession has a different story. Values are not "in a position of selecting actions. They are far too abstract and, from the standpoint of action situations, always take the form of a conflict of values."[1] They lack "the ability to form media-specific functional systems (such as science). Their directive value is low because no value can determine an act or even, as we might say with Pascal, excuse an act."[2] Nevertheless, even when Niklas Luhmann talks about the impotence of values, he has to make recourse to a value, the "directive value." But that doesn't stop him from making the sober diagnosis that it's "hardly possible to find a firm footing in ethics," which is why "one seeks to absorb uncertainty from uncoordinable, continual irritation at the level of 'values'."[3] "In themselves, values are in the first place preferences. Only through complex historical shifts in meaning have social demands also been built into the value concept since the nineteenth century."[4] But these demands don't seem to have the shaping force that the politicians emphatically attribute to them. For sociologists too, values are clearly something that resist the direct, formative access of the individual. They seem to populate a domain that protects them—that tabooizes their validity. "Values are assumed in communication, sometimes also co-communicated, but not subjected to communication."[5] The real problem, however, is their contradictory diversity: If values are in competition, they neutralize each other—preventing decisions.

The politician will contradict the sociologist by saying: "While it may well be the case that values enter into conflicts, that quite clearly doesn't prevent action. To see that, you only need to consider that still today, and perhaps today above all, it's action that determines our reality. And if the sociologist with his system theory wants to make 'action' disappear, to replace it with 'communication,' that changes nothing. In every concrete situation that leads to an action, things clearly manage to get beyond the paralyzing antagonism of values. Since it's something that happens, as opposed to nothing, no other conclusion is possible than that ultimately a value motivates the actor and initiates the action. In another situation, that prevents neither the same actor nor another one from being influenced by another value to perform another action. The values conflict and neutralization thesis might be correct in the sterile environment of sociological theory, but it doesn't cut it in practice."

If we allow the politician and the sociologist thus to come to blows, values power and values impotence remain irreconcilable. But perhaps this is a false alternative, and it befits this chapter to investigate what values can and have—and the next chapter to investigate what gets done to values. If they're not simply nothing, they must do or have something. If values are supposed not just to be but to move something, to change something in the world, that means validity is ascribed to them, and a particular kind of validity at that. This validity differs from the validity of mathematical or physical laws in that it's conceived of as determining action. Values that apply are not simply noticed, like mathematical or physical laws, but bring about particular actions (or the deliberate forgoing of action[6]) and a particular kind of living. Validity of values is thus a capacity to give direction to the doing and leaving-undone of human beings. If one attributes a power of motivation to values, that means that the actors are ready to subordinate other possible motives for their actions. So much for theory. But how does the motivating power of values look in practice?

The first idea to push itself to the surface is that values owe their motivating power to a lack—a lack that strives for compensation, for redress. Peter Sloterdijk (b. 1947) once suggested that social cohesion is owed to communal, shared worry.[7] It follows from this, he argued, that shared values drew life from the fact or fiction of shared worries—about something that affects the whole of the values-sharing group. Some people share the worry that the sea from whose fish they live or on whose shores they swim is being destroyed by pollution. They make conservation of the environment into a shared value. Others share the worry that mass lay-offs will cause severe social upheavals. For them, social peace is the shared value. The snag here is that the shared values only last as long as the worry is shared. The shared values have the task of assuaging the worry and motivating their holders to action that removes the worries, or the cause of the worries. If all potential sea-polluters are persuaded of the need for conservation and thus avoid any behavior that harms the sea, the worry about the sea gradually subsides. And why not, when it seems to be safe now? If the communal worry disappears, cohesion also starts to crumble and the shared values erode. It may well be that coast-dwellers and fisher-folk will always emphasize, if asked, how the importance of concern for the ecological balance of the sea still remains and how much they feel a duty to uphold ecological values. But the worry is now abstract, because there's no longer a threat. The ecological values no longer generate an action-motivating force. Values born of worry are therefore unstable if the worry isn't permanent. In affluent societies, worry about social cohesion becomes less salient; the corresponding invocations of values often sound hollow, because they're no longer oriented around real needs and worries.

In the worry model of society, therefore, the wise thing for social technologists and technocrats to do is prolong worries in order to ensure a long-term shared basis for life and a "values foundation." The mass media, for example, is a perfect machine for worry-production. We wouldn't know about most of the worries we have if we hadn't read about them in the newspaper or heard about them on television or the Internet. Incidentally, that doesn't mean that the media's "content creators" have been bought by the social technocrats of the state and that a vast conspiracy is behind the "mainstream media." Worries create a cohesion of concern and interest, making them the most sellable good you can imagine. It would be foolish and bad for business if the mass media were to try selling something other than worries (insight, for example, or understanding). By selling worries, which we all make into our shared concerns, the media makes a significant contribution to preventing our society crumbling into individual worrying. And we're so avid for what the mass media serves us that we want to participate in the shared worries.

There's an alternative to this idea of the motivating power of values emerging from lack, from worry. It says that values owe their motivating power to a surplus. Abbé Ferdinando Galiani (1728–1787) thought "la vertu est un enthousiasme," "virtue is an enthusiasm."[8] The values could flow from this enthusiasm like a wide river of milk and honey; they would pour out like a flood toward any corner of the globe inhabited by humans. Admittedly, if enthusiasm for the good and the just was a natural, primordial phenomenon, we would hardly need values anymore—we would submit to the enthusiasm and unstintingly do whatever it compelled us to. Or would the function of values in this event be to channel action rather than to motivate it? Would they have to ensure that the enthusiasm spreading out in all directions gained a goal and a form? Values as administrators not of the moral deficit but of the moral surplus?

Under earthly conditions, overflowing moral enthusiasm isn't the norm. Any investigation into what the situation with values would be if this were the case can happily be postponed until that distant and improbable day when moral enthusiasm comes to predominate. And until then we can advise the moral-enthusiast minority to curb and direct their moral enthusiasm via concrete values selections.

Rudolf Carnap understood value judgments as disguised instructions. Value judgments of the type "killing is evil," he believed, pretended to be empirical principles, predicating propositions, but couldn't be empirically verified. Rather, they took on the garb of a proposition to express a mere wish: "a value statement is nothing else than a command in a misleading grammatical form. It may have effects upon the actions of men, and these effects may either be in accordance with our wishes or not; but it is neither true nor false. It does not assert anything and can neither be proved nor disproved."[9] You might think Carnap's worry that value judgments might be misunderstood as empirical claims about specific situations in the world is overblown, because the people addressed by such sentences clearly react differently than to declarative sentences such as: "This tree is green." The addressees work out without any very demanding hermeneutic operations that a sentence like "Killing is evil" isn't a description of empirical reality but an injunction to avoid killing at all costs. However, interpreting all value judgments as direct injunctions or orders might cause difficulties. If you formulate a value judgment that freedom is a central value, you're clearly not issuing the order "Be free!". If you understand every last value as an order, you're missing something. Only in exceptional cases do values tell us bluntly and directly what we should do. If we take values as fictional entities, as something created by people for people, we're well advised to ascribe them a manifold mode of operation rather than a simple one.

Alfred Jules Ayer (1910–1989) conceptualizes values statements, or "ethical terms," as being, firstly, statements about emotional states. And, secondly, they serve not only to express feelings but also to produce feelings, "and so to stimulate action." In his example "It is your duty to tell the truth," it's easy to hear the order "Tell the truth!" But in the sentence "It is good to tell the truth," the order is greatly weakened, Ayer observes, and little more than a suggestion.[10]

Values are (embedded into) human communication. Since human communication can be highly varied, the effect of values, and of value expressions, will also be highly varied. To stay with the example of freedom as a value: What kind of feeling is being expressed by someone who proclaims this value? What feelings are they triggering with their proclamation? The feeling felt by the Marlboro Man when he lights a cigarette? The feeling felt by the Wall Street gambler when he sells his share package at a profit?

It's certainly correct that values, when made explicit, trigger something—in that realm known alternatively as "human interiority," "soul," "spirit," or "will." But to qualify that which is triggered as simply "feeling" might be inadequate—especially as in everyday language feelings are held to be something short-lived and transient. Moreover, values clearly don't principally aim at short-term, transient, individual actions. If I avow "It is good to tell the truth," I don't want my interlocutor to tell the truth only in this moment but, if possible, always. So should values produce a particular habitus and attitude that steers all future actions? But what is the habitus that follows from the value of freedom? Sitting in front of your computer punctually at seven in the morning to check the performance of your share packages? Or being in the stable at the same time to get your horse ready for the open range?

The term *habitus* remains as imprecise as the term *values*. Nevertheless: Values aim for permanence, not for momentary stimulation of action and feeling. Does that make the conscience into the court of instance that values could address—by provoking pangs of conscience and causing guilty consciences in order, finally, to enjoy a radiantly clean conscience? But the conscience too is no natural phenomenon; it has a history, and a very modern one that played out while the "norm-setting classes" were working via "discourses of the 'inner mission'" towards a particular goal: "all people should have a conscience."[11] A new state of affairs, therefore, because in the early modern era it was by no means the case that all people saw themselves as holders of such a thing as a conscience. Which is why, in a rare example of agreement between orthodox theologists and Enlightenment philosophers, a conscience had to be made for them. The project was successful, even beyond the misty peaks of secularization and the pluralization of religious worldviews, so that today everyone believes they have a conscience—the people who lack consciences are always the *others*, although they themselves naturally don't believe themselves conscienceless. And yet the moment of the norm-setting classes' ubiquitous success in implanting a conscience into every human individual seemed to coincide with the decline of their norm-setting powers. From now on, every person could believe themselves accountable only to their own conscience, not to anyone else. Conscience as internal property, as the driving force of individualization and atomization of humanity?

Conscience as internal property, as an inner court of last instance to which everyone is entitled? This is a modern invention rather than a gift of nature. Values, at least known as such, only came onto the scene when the conscience had already become generally established. Was it the norm-setting classes who thought up values in order to win back control over the conscience, which seemed to be able to escape control so easily? Or was it the emancipated conscience-holders themselves who invented values and their plurality in order to ensure their autonomy, each conscience-holder authorizing their own values quantum at their own discretion? Values as tokens that keep the conscience machine running—like a jukebox or a roulette wheel? What comes out of the machine, what music is played, the amount of the winnings or losses, is hard to predict. The values tokens fed into the conscience can yield all manner of effects, but seldom predictable ones.

One observer notes that the values tokens activate the conscience as a self-verification mechanism: I have values; I follow them in my actions, so I have a good conscience, even if the world abhors my actions. Someone else realizes with horror that the values tokens stimulate a bad conscience because the values can never be lived up to; their validity claims can never be fully satisfied in the conscience-holder's actions. For this self-observer, values cause guilt—the feeling that you can never live up to them. This self-observer will feel vindicated by a book such as David Graeber's (1961–2020) *Debt. The First 5000 Years*, which sets out to show how the modern human languishes under the yoke of debt that can never be repaid. We have to take on debt, Graeber argues, if we want to lead a life not restricted to mere survival.[12] And these debts push the majority of humanity into servitude that no one can ever free them from. Economic debts are converted into moral debt, or guilt, in order to eternalize this servitude. Only a radical debt cancellation and overcoming of capitalism could free humanity from the vicious circle of economic debts and moral guilt.

But is the self-observer of conscience-tormenting values and moralized debts not succumbing to utopian wishful thinking? This pipe dream comes in two parts, the first depicting the situation of the contemporary human as entirely downtrodden, indebted, guilt-ridden, in other words: requiring redemption. The second, following on from this, recommends the protagonist as a class-war Messiah sweeping away all poverty and bringing salvation. Is it not the case that in Western societies even the poorest have things that even rich elites in earlier centuries could not have dreamt of? No one must starve, and almost no one is denied a warm bed, a smartphone or a television. Debt peonage has been abolished; private insolvency enables anyone to start anew and thumb their noses at their creditors. Not being able to repay debts has long since stopped being a social disgrace, with the result that even a multiple bankrupt like Donald Trump could become US president, while any honorable businessman in his situation a century ago would have seen no alternative but to blow his own brains out. "For the Ancients, non-payment of debts was one of the most damnable transgressions—a crime of omission of abysmal turpitude."[13]

It may well be the case that private and public debts have grown exponentially. But that doesn't necessarily mean that the yoke of these debts has become heavier, that the debt regime is now stricter. In an age in which economic debts have been universalized, they no longer leave the bitter aftertaste of moral guilt. "In this context, it is possible to ascertain what the modern age means from the perspective of the history of morality. It increasingly emancipates the debtor, especially major debtors, from persecution by creditors and exculpates the social failure from his own guilt. More than that, the imposition of suffering as retribution for unpaid debts is deplored; the bankrupt escapes painlessly; there is no longer any compensation through suffering. If it is the state that over-borrows to the point of bankruptcy, it is even said that the creditor, not the debtor, is guilty."[14] What Peter Sloterdijk noted a few years ago is currently being confirmed in the situation of chronically broke states such as Greece, which is not only allowed to defer its debts continuously but is also continuously being granted new loans, even though it's clear to everyone that it will never be able to repay them. And all this is done with liberal reference to "shared values." The values drawn on here are intended not to produce a guilty conscience but more to suggest that modern values-morality has done away with the logic of guilt and retribution. Values simply count for more than any number of accumulated debts.

The macro-political deferral of credit for states and corporations, like the micro-political relief of individuals' debts via social security, could be seen as strong indicators that what has often theatrically been decried as the economization of our lifeworld is merely a pious if highly effective fairytale.

To the layperson, it might seem as if doing away with the logic of debt and retribution, such that debtors no longer make their repayments because no one can or does force them to, would very quickly lead to systemic collapse. But this notion is probably naive, because the two defining principles of the debt economy are, firstly, the concentration of capital, so that rich creditors don't really suffer if they don't get their repayments and, secondly, inflation. Running in parallel to any deferral of debt repayments is the continuous depreciation of the substance of the debt. One hundred deutschmarks might have been a substantial debt in 1966, requiring many days of work to pay off, but, converted to 50 euros in today's money, the sum is enough for little more than dinner and a bus ride home. The tendency of debt to disappear over time distinguishes it from guilt which, at least in the traditional conception, no time can heal—which in fact actually grows over time, like original sin, because it gives birth to further guilt.

It's clear that values, by contrast, don't primarily serve a public that organizes its reality into categories of guilt and sin or of debt and repayment. If you want to press values thought into this schema, you must do one of two things: either turn everyone indiscriminately into debtors—the values demand tribute, recognition from all—regardless of what we otherwise have or don't have. Or the values thought dissolves every concrete loan obligation because everyone participates equally in values. The precious asset is now values; not that which I can lend to others and which as a creditor I aim to get back in the form of interest—and values are neither reduced if more people participate in them nor do they increase with interest and compound interest. They can neither be lent nor collected. Recoverability is, nevertheless, a defining feature of debt morality.

The values boom may indicate that the economic logic of debt and retribution no longer pertains. Values thought as the expression of a de-economization of the modern lifeworld? Contrary to initial suspicions, values evoke in principle neither a bad conscience nor guilt. People who believe themselves to be guided by values feel justified regardless of whether their values-guided actions have met with success or not. A law, an imperative, by contrast, knows only *pass or fail*. Either you did what you were commanded to do or you didn't. And if you didn't do it, no justification that you were acting in the spirit of the law but didn't quite manage to complete the task will do. You'll remain a failure and earn a guilty conscience. Values, by contrast, were invented by people *precisely because they didn't want to have a guilty conscience*. Values are ideal means of exculpation and excuse, which incidentally proves that all the talk of the economization of the lifeworld was merely a *bien pensant* fad rather than an all-defining reality. Values release us from all guilt; they're the moral debt relief package of choice. It seems as if the encroachments of economics aren't quite as severe and as all-present as some would have us believe.

To say, therefore, that the court of the conscience (in any case an ominous locale) is the place where values take effect, where they become active, causes some problems. Is it not simpler to return to the old idea that values are nothing more than wishes or preferences that are acted out? The Canadian philosopher Charles Taylor (b. 1931) has raised an objection to the simplistic equation of values with wishes. A person has a great many wishes that are born from particular moments and dictated by momentary needs. In this moment I can prefer a slice of Black Forest gateau to a slice of Linzer Torte. This preference, which might be reversed in the space of an hour, is itself not a value. But people can have wishes of a higher, second order, "strong evaluations," which help them to organize and regulate their everyday first-order wishes, indeed, to have them or not to have them. Such a second-order wish reflects on the first-order wishes and tests their justification. If I have a second-order wish to lead a healthy life, I might reject the first-order wish for cake, abjure both the Black Forest gateau and the Linzer Torte and eat a salad. Second-order wishes can condition the first-order values. For Taylor, it's values that ultimately decide what kind of people we are, what kind of life we lead.[15] In this scenario, the strong evaluations or values exert an assertive, decisive influence on my life, and what values do would be of major importance.

But we are the ones who call these values into life in the very first place. We are the ones who grant them power over our lives. Values are regulative fictions that we create and that we choose. Here there's a whiff of the sweat-soaked pathos of an existential self-selection: I define myself as who I want to be—and I do so by defining my values. Self-selection is values-selection. Charles Taylor, however, if asked, would relieve this self-selection pathos of its lead weight and clouds of incense, because he doesn't imagine some isolated individual on a lonely summit making existential decisions for herself. His concern is with working out how, in our strong evaluations, we are bound into a community of other people. According to Taylor, our values depend on the values that are pre-inscribed into a culture. We must draw on the values patterns and speech modes that are already there in order to integrate ourselves socially. The values are communicated to us and at most we can adapt them to our own needs, but we don't conjure them out of nothing. We can't choose values like cakes.

We are—and here I agree with Taylor—embedded within values structures; we're not sovereign, values-defining individuals. This might seem morose, because it shows that our freedom is a highly restricted one, if it doesn't even extend to sovereignly setting our own values. And it explains why someone like Nietzsche found the highest promise of happiness and freedom in the "transvaluing of all values": the promise of mastery over oneself, one's own world, and thus of one's own values. In an empirical world, however, in which finite individuals are bound to time- and space-related conditions, this promise can't be cashed in.

Taylor's schema of first- and second-order evaluations is based on the preference model of his American colleague Harry G. Frankfurt (b. 1929). Sonja Feger, following on from Frankfurt, also defined value as "preference of the significance of pre-reflexive preference": After Frankfurt, she argued, it's not possible to define something as significant and at the same time remain indifferent to this attribution of significance.[16] So even an attribution of significance itself seems significant. According to Feger, a person who prefers friendship to non-friendship is attributing significance not only to friendship but also to their preference for the significance of friendship. If so, on our search for the location of value, we would already have reached a third-order level. On the first level would be my preference for friendship with Michael, Agatha, or Thomas; on the second, my conviction that friendship in general is a good thing; and on the third level—which would thus be the "actual" value level—would be my preference for considering the second-level conviction significant and thus granting it a life-guiding power. You can see the problem: Taylor's two levels aren't enough, because Level 2 would have to be differentiated internally and can't be adequately described with "strong evaluation." But if we undertake this differentiation, Level 3 won't satisfy us and we'll have to keep bringing in new levels for housing the values-content of the respective previous layers.

There are practical advantages to the fact that, as soon as one sets foot on the field, one postulates second-order wishes that structure, organize, and focus the immediate wishes of the first order. It's just that these second-order wishes are in no way necessary or even of primarily moral nature (assuming one knows what "moral nature" is). A second-order wish might be to become rich or powerful. The first-order wishes would then be organized in line with this. I happily concede to Taylor that these second-order wishes lie outside of my free choice, being instead subject to socio-cultural shaping forces that I don't control. Admittedly, if we take these strong individual-wish-defining evaluations as the expression of our sense for what is valuable or relevant or fulfilling,[17] it seems difficult to follow Taylor in judging the larger truthfulness and appropriateness of these evaluations without introducing a kind of philosophical super-censorship, which would have to be placed on a third level, to the effect, for example, that the second-order wish for wealth is inferior to one for an altruistic new direction in life.

Demands for philosophical super-censorship would seem worthy of a certain mistrust. On this third, reflexive level, the individual or the philosopher would be dealing with the correction of false second-level wishes. I don't deny that this philosophical super-censorship is a possibility, but it would itself be an obstacle to moral values-stability, because it's pre-programmed with regress to lower levels. And ultimately is it really the reflecting philosophical conscience that decides what is considered valuable, or rather the prevailing local prejudice, the particular social and cultural consensus? In modern Western societies, for example, altruism is more highly rated in this consensus than individual self-enrichment. If so, values are social implants that guide the self-interpretation of individuals. This is a move away from the superstition that morality is in the first instance to do with interiority, the unsullied *ought*, the self-imposed duty of pure practical reason. Morality is based not on self-legislation of a sincere, good, and entirely free will. In morality, what matters is not what I am for myself or what I really am (assuming for purposes of argument that there is such a "reality"), the "nature" and "core" of the human. On the contrary, morality is perhaps the most external thing of all about humans (also, incidentally, about other animals). Morality as a means of determining the outer world, of negotiating the borders. The converse view might be nothing more than a perspectival and moral deception that has produced the millennia-old habit of writing morality ever-deeper into the human, as the interiorization of a conditioning, a domestication (or a cruelty), thanks to which morality came to function more smoothly.

And values? Are they mere vehicles of morality, because the supposedly free will is clearly too weak for autonomy? Does free will need values as training wheels? If so, it would be neither entirely free nor self-legislating. Are values thus the expression of the shameful insight that morality has nothing to do with interior life or with a duty-bound and reason-driven autonomy? Are they merely rules and regulations for dealing with that which is not *I*? Do we thus set them up as exterior determinants, as border guards hypostatized into autonomous entities?

Some will respond to the insight that morality is a universal, public business rather than a personal, individual one (this is by no means a new insight) by concluding that there must be another interior space, one that is sealed off from this morality that wages wars of conquest with values as weapons; there must be a realm of self-legislation untouched by this morality. This is the soul as air-raid shelter against moral impositions, a fortification against values armaments. Some believe we have to distinguish in principle between morality and individual ethics. Morality, they say, is about the general good, while individual ethics is about personal happiness or self-actualization. This distinction would, however, only be a distinction in principle if people really were completely independent, individual beings, individual subjects, standing opposite an exterior world as "homines clausi."[18] But a person is never only a person in and for themself, they are always that which they are in relation and through relation. So it seems somewhat naive to have morality turn back, as it were, at the front door of the individual, who is then ascribed an autarchic interior life. One could postulate that morality is the means by which society colonizes the individual. And the values are the air power and the boots on the ground that enforce this colonization. In modernity, moral colonization is all-encompassing. There is no longer any function system that is untouched by morality. Values are always along for the ride.

When the American philosopher Richard Rorty (1931–2007) describes this pragmatism as being, among other things, an attitude that relinquishes any metaphysical difference between facts and values, he does so because he locates the shared core of scholarship and morality in deliberation, in the weighing-up and consideration of various alternatives, in an equality of processes.[19] Language is the medium that equalizes values and facts in this way. This would make the ways in which values and facts function impossible in principle to distinguish from each other.

One objection to this would be that a stone has a different penetrative power than a value. You only have to compare how differently a stone and a value affect a windowpane—the first with explosive force; the second not at all. To which Rorty might respond that, firstly, the fact is not the stone itself but only the observed and linguistically articulated process, for example: "Now a stone is flying through the living room window." Secondly, if the stone itself were a fact, it would still in no way follow from this particular fact that every fact has a penetrative power similar to that of the stone. The fact "cotton wool," for example, would not. So the claimed difference between values and facts couldn't lie in penetrative power.

In the light of all this, we might be willing to concede Rorty's point, less because we agree with his notion of speech acts and more because in a morally colonized world we can no longer even imagine any facts that don't have moral connotations. However many counterexamples the physicists can list, any so-called facts from the domains in which people deal with people can always have a moral reading.

But there may be resistance to such a capitulation to morality. Just because facts may be interpreted morally doesn't mean that they *must* be interpreted morally. Is it not more reasonable to assume that most facts that people have to deal with are in the first instance morally indifferent and are only loaded with morality in retrospect—in the attempt to gain primacy over their interpretation and definition via values? The result is that even a walk in the countryside is no longer morally neutral but rather an affirmation of ecological sustainability, and paying your plumber by bank transfer rather than cash is an act of protest against tax-dodging. The moral mode of viewing the world isn't a necessity of nature. It would be taking the thesis of moral colonization too far to claim that morality was indiscriminately assimilating everything and that all resistance to it was futile. It may well be worth trialing tactics of apatheticization; these might not be able to restore facts to their pre-moral innocence, but they might strongly reduce their values-chargedness. Like toxic chemicals, values should be subject to compulsory environmental impact assessment.

You might regard values as facts or as vehicles of moral rearmament; you might introduce a hierarchy of preferences; you might hold values responsible for a guilty conscience or a spotless one; you might regard them as expressions of feelings or means of production of feeling or, ultimately, see them as compensators for faults. But in every case, each impact and effect can also be produced by non-values. If values evoke feelings, so too can being in love; if values can be understood as orders, then so too can assembly instructions; if values make consciences, so too do setbacks; if values form the self, so too can principles or socio-economic pressures. And how do actions that are in context with values, that are motivated by values, differ from those that aren't? If I blow my nose, am I inspired by the value of health or the value of cleanliness? In which of my actions am I governed by values? Whatever values are capable of, they don't seem to be exclusively capable of it.

Moral rearmament can also be achieved through threats, or enthusiasm, or flattery. If someone now objects that values are also somewhere behind all these threats or flatteries, that the values use these threats or flatteries to make themselves felt, then that someone might be rescuing the exclusive having, doing, and being-able-to of values, at least for a moment. But the price for this is high: The price is a world in which values are ubiquitous and pervasive—a world in which a value lurks behind every guileless phenomenon, just waiting to self-actualize. In this view of reality, almost nothing exists except values and their disguises. World events become a struggle between values, one that's never resolved because values don't interact harmoniously with each other but fight for primacy and existence. The value of utility maximization contradicts the value of humility; the value of profit stands against that of self-denial. The values that seem to exert the greatest efficacy seem to be the ones that no one wants to openly own up to—the shamefully concealed and disguised ones: love of money and thirst for power, for example. Or is there some reason why those should not be values? Just because many of us execrate them?

A world consisting only of values and their wars would be an unbearable one—a world that offered nowhere to rest because its inhabitants would have to be ceaselessly engaged in evaluation of everything and every fellow inhabitant. If such a world did exist, it would be worthy of abolition.

It's more cheerful to assume the world is in fact much more than a comfortless values-fabric. The world of the values realist is a different world from that of the happy person. To reinvent the world as values-fabric simply in order to rescue the having, doing, and being-able-to of values, is an act of desperation. Better, surely, to content oneself with values as something made by people for people. Even as communicative entities of this kind, they remain, like other human products, facts in their own right—not because they exist somewhere out there but because they exist with and in us, in our communication. To point out these are shadowy, fleeting facts without clear outlines isn't to say they're not facts; it casts doubt only on their substantiality in a conventional metaphysical sense. But we human beings also lack such substantiality.

So what is it that values exclusively have, do, and are capable of? What they're capable of, what they do, and how they differ from the traditional good: They connect unconnected things with each other. They achieve—as regulative fictions—the connection of domains that previously seemed to have nothing to do with each other. The value of freedom, for example, enmeshes politics with economics, individual autonomy with group-interest. Or, the value of self-denial enmeshes religion with ecology, heteronomy with transcendence of the ego. Modern societies invented values because of their capacity to amalgamate. After tirelessly differentiating themselves, these societies have formed countless function areas that no longer seem to be in contact with each other. It's now values that are tasked with producing connections between them. Connections that are more than chance, fleeting touches. The promise of values is their amalgamating power—the power to connect unconnected things with each other. They're supposed to join many realities together to make one reality. They can only do that provisionally and situatively—because there are so many of them and at the same time they're highly mutable.

Precisely because of their diversity and susceptibility to change, values are typical children of modernity. While they connect the unconnected realms of contemporary life, they do so not definitively but in constantly new and different ways. Values cope with the dynamism that characterizes modernity by being themselves dynamic rather than rigid, in the manner of sacred principles, irrevocable doctrines, or social dictates. The amalgamation permits every possible hybrid relationship; the amalgamation is performed by incessant calibrating and weighing-up. The hybrid relationships of values and those of reality are completely different from each other—and in a world of movement, they have to be. Moral values creation functions through amalgamation.

The amalgamation of different domains by means of values doesn't only reduce complexity. At the same time, it also multiplies the complexity, because the possible amalgams of values and realities are endless. A functionalist social scientist might want to understand values as cultural exhaust filters, designed to reduce pollution levels in social interaction. But the problem here is the same as in the automotive industry: If you cut back on one pollutant, you increase the others. Values conflicts continuously summon up new conflicts. While some values throttle back the general busyness machine in order to guarantee a healthy paralysis, at least for a while, other values are indomitable sources of movement and a reservoir of motivation to action. They can only be connected for moments. And perhaps that's not such a bad thing after all.

Notes

1. Niklas Luhmann: Die Gesellschaft der Gesellschaft. Frankfurt a. M. 1997, vol. 1, p. 341.
2. Ibid., p. 344.
3. Ibid., vol. 2, p. 798.
4. Ibid., p. 799.
5. Ibid.

6. Often not to act does indeed seem the correct moral path; see Henning Ottmann (ed.): Negative Ethik. Berlin 2005 and Henning Ottmann/ Stefano Saracino/Peter Seyferth (eds.): Gelassenheit. Und andere Versuche zur negativen Ethik. Berlin/Munich 2014.
7. See Peter Sloterdijk: Zeilen und Tage. Notizen 2008–2011. Frankfurt a. M. 2012, p. 218.
8. Ferdinando Galiani: Lettres à Madame d'Épinay, Voltaire, Diderot, Grimm, le Baron d'Holbach, Morellet, Suart, D'Alembert, Marmontel, la Vicomtesse de Belsunce etc. Publiées d'après les éditions originales augmentées des variantes, de nombreuses notes et d'un index avec notice biographique par Eugène Asse. Paris 1882, vol. 2, p. 276 (letter to Madame d'Épinay dated April 26, 1777).
9. Rudolf Carnap: Philosophy and Logical Syntax. London 1935, p. 24.
10. Alfred Jules Ayer: Language, Truth and Logic. 2nd edition. New York 1952, p. 108.
11. Heinz D. Kittsteiner: Die Entstehung des modernen Gewissens. Frankfurt a. M. 1995, p. 17.
12. David Graeber: Debt. The First 5000 Years. Brooklyn, NY 2011, p. 379.
13. Sloterdijk: Zeilen und Tage, p. 610.
14. Ibid.
15. See Charles Taylor: Human Agency and Language. Philosophical Papers 1. Cambridge/London/New York 1985, pp. 23–26.
16. See Harry G. Frankfurt: The Importance of What We Care About. Philosophical Essays. Cambridge/New York 1988, p. 92.
17. Taylor: Human Agency and Language, p. 38.
18. Norbert Elias: Über die Einsamkeit der Sterbenden in unseren Tagen. Frankfurt a. M. 1982, p. 81.
19. Richard Rorty: Consequences of Pragmatism (Essays: 1972–1980). Minneapolis 1982, p. 163 f.

CHAPTER 9

An Unruly Victim Tamed. What Things Are Done to Values?

Abstract This chapter, "An Unruly Victim Tamed" explores the dynamic nature of human values and their susceptibility to external influences. Drawing a parallel between celestial mechanics and moral mechanics, the chapter examines how values have evolved over time, narrowing their orbit around humanity and fragmenting into a rotating ring of ideals. The discourse delves into the malleability of values, challenging the notion of fixed, unchanging substances. It questions the control and influence over values, analyzing the interplay between subjects and the values they uphold. The chapter discusses philosophical perspectives, including Nietzsche's concept of transvaluation and Nozick's value ethics. It highlights the auction principle that pervades modern society, where values are negotiable and subject to rapid fluctuations. The narrative acknowledges the complexity of values administration, their adaptability, and the need for responsible handling. Ultimately, the chapter emphasizes the importance of understanding and effectively managing the fluid and evolving nature of values in contemporary life.

Keywords Values evolution • Celestial mechanics analogy • Subjectification of the good • Transvaluation • Auction principle • Values administration • Fluidity of values • Nietzschean philosophy • Nozick's value ethics • Dynamic nature of values

A. U. Sommer, *Values*,
https://doi.org/10.1007/978-3-031-42159-4_9

In a few million years, the moon Phobos will have gotten so close to its home planet Mars it will disintegrate. At this point, the debris may coalesce and form a ring, which will then encircle Mars in place of the satellite.

Celestial mechanics seem to imitate moral mechanics. Over the centuries, the good has been describing an ever-narrower orbit around the human world—this is what is meant by the "subjectification of the good"—leading ultimately to its fragmentation into myriad lumps of rock which now, as values, process in a rotating ring of rubble around the human world. The collapsing moon and the collapsing good share a twin fate.

If you ask what values are, what they do, and what they're capable of, you shouldn't forget that they too are subject to influences—like the moon, attracted by Martian gravity, or like the good, succumbing to the pull of subjectifying gravity. At any rate, this is what we are compelled to accept if we don't see values as existing entirely in and for themselves as unchanging substances in a domain of absolute seclusion. If they're subject to change, there must be things that are done to them. But what is done to them, and by whom?

The counter-question poses itself: What happens to people who are subject to values? Not only to those who surrender themselves to values like profit maximization but also to those who uphold the values of self-denial or reclusion? The social and psychological history of values-based developmental trauma remains to be written. Let's leave both this question and the counter-question to the historians. Values passion tales would be gripping, but they're not our subject.

If things can be done to values, then values must be something, although perhaps only something that we produce when we speak or think. And when we feel. And when we want. Even as speech about values emerged in the nineteenth century, a consciousness was forming in some places that values were neither untouchable substances, existing for themselves, nor things that only correlate with other values, but rather that it's people who make their own values. "The fundamental belief of metaphysicians is the *belief in the oppositions of values*,"[1] remarked Nietzsche, challenging this faith in rock-hard values with his intention to bring about "transvaluation." No to metaphysicians, therefore, but yes to philosophers, or at least new philosophers: The "task" of such a philosopher "demands that he creates values."[2] By this he doesn't mean economic values—there was much discussion at the time about the way these were created through labor. Instead, Nietzsche takes this contemporary rhetoric at its word, generalizes it, and ascribes to a selected intellectual elite the capacity to produce moral values—the values that are supposed to determine life as a whole. His philosopher of the future is expected to also be an artist and legislator; one who must set the standards according to which a society has to organize itself. Sadly, however, he doesn't reveal to his readers how this philosopher is supposed to achieve all this. By writing books? By deciding to become a politician? By making himself into a secular high priest? And, if he is to transvalue existing values and create new ones, does he not in turn need values of a higher order to be guided by? Who is in control of the values? Whom do the values control?

The Nietzschean preoccupation with transvaluation has faded away. But the problem of how we gain the upper hand over values that seem to have the upper hand over us remains. Even avowedly anarchist and libertarian thinkers such as Robert Nozick (1938–2002) have a hard time subordinating the values to entirely human control. For him, the human appears as a "value-seeker"[3] who doesn't create values themselves but has to grasp them in order for them to become effective: "Values themselves lack causal powers."[4] As soon as we've chosen, we've voluntarily placed ourselves under their command: "We know what value would be; we have only to bring it to life, to value it, to seek and pursue it, contouring our lives in accordance with it."[5] In contrast to Charles Taylor, in Nozick's model we're not simply subjected as social beings to values but, as autonomous beings, approach them in a relationship of decision and choice, precisely because values, of themselves, aren't capable of exerting any causal power that might be able to compel us to make such a choice. But as soon as we realize them in our life (Nozick calls this "realizationism"[6]), their yardstick applies unrestrictedly to us. Nozick's value ethics thus wants to rescue both the autonomy of the subject and the non-madeness of values; it attempts to do so by thinking of subjects and values, at least ideal-typically, as initially being independent of each other before finding their way to each other in the subject's act of choosing.

Admittedly, this model does pose some problems. Firstly, the subject's freedom to choose in some pre-values state is a visibly counter-factual assumption, because without a values-choice taking place to determine values—that is, an already-premised evaluation of values—it's impossible to see why subjects should decide on values. This would at least mean that the value of approving of values would have a causal power that would constrain the freedom of the subject—who is strangely isolated in this conception—right from the start. If we then grasp and realize values, they are subjected to a transformation that makes them into something completely new, something that gains power over the choosing subject. Values and subjects have a negative effect on each other. Do the values now fall into the grasp of the subjects or do the subjects fall into the grasp of the values?

Nozick's approach—seeing values as neither completely unreal, nor pure creations of individual human willpower, nor entities that exist for themselves and that have always determined human action—has much to recommend it. But whether his realizationism adequately describes the human approach to values, the doing and being-done-to of values, remains questionable. Consider the following situation, which may get significantly closer to an adequate description of contemporary values realities: a precocious child, on the bus to elementary school, sitting next to a classmate who's attempting to buy some toy on eBay and lecturing him about how online auctions work, their potential pitfalls, and payment options. The nine-year-old has understood that in the contemporary world almost nothing has a fixed, definitively established price, but rather that this price is negotiable—and that if you're the sole bidder you can, with the right tricks, get it down below the pain barrier, but that if multiple bidders want the same item, you have to watch impotently as the price soars to exorbitant heights. Other than this nine-year-old, has anyone reflected on the eBayization of our lifeworld, in which the auction principle has become the defining maxim—the expectation that bargains are waiting to be snapped up everywhere?

It's not just things that no longer have a fixed price. Values are also being caught up in the maelstrom of negotiability. Political theoreticians politely dub this "deliberation" and act as if it comprised a giving and taking of reasons, but in reality, every participant is interested solely in emerging with the best deal. It's in particular around the so-called moral values that the auction principle has long established itself. After a catastrophe such as an earthquake or the wreck of a refugee ship, the highest bids go to compassion, sympathy, and solidarity, while a few days later—and this is particularly the case after events such as terror attacks—these are superseded in the values hierarchy by national self-assertion, depending on who is ready to stake what symbolic capital. The euphoric *Willkommenskultur* ("welcome culture") with which Germany accepted refugees in 2015 gives way overnight to apathetic disillusion, which some newspapers brand a racist response by lumpen reactionaries, a frantic attempt to maintain the values level within acceptable parameters. It remains the case that, while there's a particular group of values that are repeatedly invoked in the modern world, their exchange rate is subject to enormous fluctuations, depending on the momentary level of demand. The moral preachers among philosophers and politicians will object here that values serve for long-term orientation; they couldn't be further from mere playthings of a notoriously fickle market that hawks values to the highest bidder. One of the oldest ways of trying to prove the existence of values is to project onto them qualities of permanence and unchangingness, a strategy employed by those who espouse values but secretly fear they're a (presumably weak) replacement for the metaphysical good, beautiful, and true. If you can no longer hold on to the good, beautiful, and true on the grounds of their proven non-existence, you want the values at least to appear durable and unchanging. But this cultural-conservative rhetoric misses the fundamental thing, and the fundamentally new thing, in speech about language compared with speech about the good, beautiful, or true: The fact that values are movable, changeable, is precisely what makes them vastly superior to the rigid good, beautiful, and true. When values undergo change they don't break but become new—in daily life they're continuously being rearranged and updated.

The cultural pessimist's raised finger of condemnation and warning is misplaced: The situations in which values come into play in life change rapidly; correspondingly, a succession of changing values and continuous rebalancing of their situative utility is not only inevitable but reasonable. The nine-year-old wants to bid on toys, the thirteen-year-old on a smartphone, the twenty-two-year-old on happiness, and the eighty-two-year-old on a peaceful dotage. Human beings live in a fabric of values, a values weave that's incessantly redesigning, rearranging, and reprioritizing itself. This meets modern needs. To keep on accomplishing this rearrangement is the daily business of values administration. And this functions according to the auction principle. Sometimes empathy is the highest bidder; sometimes self-interest.

Values can and should stand up to abuse. You have to be able to stretch and bend them. That's also why we vacillate so much about what we call a "value"—and why there isn't a single even remotely binding list of values to be found in this book. There are endless possible candidates for values, which can also be grouped according to family resemblance (compassion, sympathy, empathy, helpfulness, and sensitivity, for example, have common features distinct from self-assertion, self-esteem, self-actualization, self-formation, self-conquest, self-creation, etc.), but can't then be conclusively systematized or ascribed to "fundamental values." The reason for this is, firstly, that values are and have to be elastic and flexible. And, secondly, that what makes values values is that they are considered to be and are presented as such in communication—that someone bids on them. Values-becoming is possible at all times and in all places. Even people you hate or shun cherish their own values. Racists, for example, or bloodthirsty fundamentalists. We shouldn't deny that they have values. We should ensure that their values receive the fewest possible bids in the social auction, no more than other *non-valeurs*, as financial securities that have been taken out of circulation are known. An enduringly helpful concept here is the "Test of Ridicule," propagated by the English moral philosopher Anthony Ashley-Cooper, third Earl of Shaftesbury (1671–1713),[7] in which anything passed off as untouchable and holy is submerged in the acid bath of irreverent humor in order to determine its fitness. Many values, not just those of racists and murderous fundamentalists, can't reliably pass this test.

For several decades, an entire research sector focusing exclusively on what happens to values has been establishing itself. Under the subject heading "values-transformation," survey after survey is carried out. "What is valuable to you?" is the question posed by eager social scientists, tracking marital fidelity as it drops 1.5 percent points since last year, while career advancement gains three points, and close friendships stubbornly hold their place in the low two figures. The unspoken premise of these studies is that values are in fact the product or at least the object of communication, and can, or even must, be accordingly articulated. Implicit or concealed values, that's to say, those that secretly regulate human behavior but that humans neither consciously choose nor even admit to, make no appearance in the colorful diagrams. Often, in any case, the test subjects are given a ready-made selection of values between which they must share out their points, with no option to formulate their own values preferences outside of such precepts. This makes values the object and product of communication led by values-transformation researchers. And this communication is a wonderful opportunity to insert your own values-preferences—for example, the American sociologist Ronald F. Inglehart's (b. 1934) wishful idea that "material values" were increasingly being replaced in Western societies by "post-material values."[8] Even the most orthodox values ontologist can't fail to learn from values-transformation research, especially in its highly differentiated contemporary form, that the preferences according to which individuals and groups hope to be able to design their lives, if not actually shape them in reality, have become fluid. And if we allow ourselves just for a moment to reduce preferences and values to a single category, we'll also find ourselves diagnosing a process of values fluidization.

Nevertheless, to take the fact that values are at the mercy of history, that their validity is subject to historical change, and associate this exclusively with fluidization, would be to consider only one side of the problem. Historicization means not just fluidization but also sedimentation, concretion. History not only makes things liquid, it also makes them solid. Far from only dissolving, rupturing, it also cements. In time, duration joins and binds. This is a helpful reminder to those who see history only as the great destroyer at work, lacerating like a tornado all that is safe and secure: history as the handmaid of nihilism. In fact, through duration, history creates a certain fixity, a temporary bindingness. It could thus, *pace* nihilism, be described in the words *Der Spiegel* magazine once used in a scandal-inducing report on the troubled West German armed forces: "of provisional defense readiness." The fixity and bindingness developed over history are, admittedly, only temporary. Anything more than that, however, is unrealistic to expect in this world. It seems consoling enough.

For some, it's tempting to pass on hastily, too hastily, from the suffering of values to the values of suffering. Christianity, for example, emphasized the value of suffering as a way of following the suffering Redeemer. Perhaps it still does, if it represents a serious alternative to mere affirmation of the earthly realm and hasn't yet evaporated in a haze of wellbeing and niceness platitudes. Today there are some scattered trends toward secularized values of suffering. For example, there's a tendency observed by historian Jan Plamper (b. 1970) among Germans to fancy themselves victims of World War II, firstly of the bombing of German cities, then the alleged mass rapes by Allied soldiers, and ending up with grandchildren of the war generation justifying their own failure as the result of ancestral trauma. Self-victimization begins where no positive hero-role remains.[9] The victim, and not just in the self-sacrifice of the suicide bomber, gains a new presence, unexpectedly giving new nourishment to the old suspicion that a slave-morality transvaluation is taking place.[10] Is it the symptom of a culture in its final stages, no longer capable of action, when suffering rather than doing becomes the center of things?[11] From all sides, today, we hear of "wounds" inflicted by one's love life, one's boss, exploitative capitalism, or a mean kindergarten teacher. If this kind of speech is to be believed, an epidemic of damage-obsession is raging. The lower the threat of real, visible wounds in a social milieu, the more this damage-obsession escalates. No previous culture has ever kept the threshold of objective, physical injury as low as it is in contemporary Europe. And no other culture dwells so intensively on subjective, psychological injuries. Here, everyone has a right to their own trauma history. A life without psychological wounds seems a hopelessly bleak one. But it would be premature to take a handful of indicators and blow them up into a comprehensive theory of modernity. Which doesn't mean that one should stop observing the newly rampant desire for suffering and incurring injury. Humans are mish-mash beings. They don't simply run a genetic program; the program itself is changed by its "environment," its "milieu," its "culture." Being human means distilling, just for a while, a unity from one's own mish-mash. And everyone does this differently. Every individual unit is perspective-bound—everyone lives partially in their own world. In their values world.

But values are often handled incorrectly—as if they were pre-existing things, rigid principles. Even though their advantage lies precisely in their dynamism, their variability, their flexibility, their capacity for having things done to them. We might "have" values, but we must learn the correct way of handling them. These are highly sensitive creatures, but they're useful for a wide range of tasks. One should not treat living creatures like Lego pieces. And values are living creatures because they spring from our living imagination.

Notes

1. Friedrich Nietzsche: Jenseits von Gut und Böse. Vorspiel einer Philosophie der Zukunft. In: ibid.: Sämtliche Werke. Kritische Studienausgabe in 15 Einzelbänden. ed. Giorgio Colli and Mazzino Montinari. 3rd ed. Munich/Berlin/New York 1999, vol. 5, pp. 9–243, here p. 16.
2. Ibid., p. 144.
3. Robert Nozick: Philosophical Explanations. Cambridge, Mass. 1981, p. 463.
4. Ibid. p. 436.
5. Ibid., p. 563.
6. Ibid., p. 556.
7. Anthony Earl of Shaftesbury: Characteristicks of Men, Manners, Opinions, Times & c. in Three Volumes. Volume I: Containing, A Letter concerning Enthusiasm. London 1733, p. 11.

8. Ronald Inglehart: The Silent Revolution. Changing Values and Political Styles among Western Publics. Princeton 1977.
9. See Jan Plamper: Die Deutschen als Opfer. In: Neue Zürcher Zeitung, 8 June 2015.
10. Friedrich Nietzsche: Zur Genealogie der Moral. Eine Streitschrift. In:Ibid.: Gesammelte Werke. Kritische Studienausgabe in 15 Einzelbänden. Eds. Giorgio Colli and Mazzino Montinari. 3rd ed. Munich/Berlin/New York 1999, vol. 5, pp. 245–412, here p. 267.
11. See also Daniele Giglioli: Die Opferfalle. Wie die Vergangenheit die Zukunft fesselt. Translated from Italian to German by Max Henninger. Berlin 2015.

CHAPTER 10

Excursus II: Values in the Political Soap Opera

Abstract This chapter, "Values in the Political Soap Opera," delves into the intricate interplay between values, politics, and society, examining the fluid and dynamic nature of values in the context of contemporary political discourse. Using examples from Angela Merkel's refugee policy to the aftermath of terrorist attacks, the chapter explores the paradoxes and ambiguities inherent in political discussions about values. It questions the fixation on preserving static values in a rapidly changing world and highlights the importance of multiple perspectives and adaptability. The chapter critiques the tendency to frame values as rigid and universally binding, arguing instead for a more nuanced understanding that embraces irony, indifference, and a diverse range of viewpoints. Ultimately, it suggests that an ironically leavened solidarity, coupled with a healthy dose of indifference, may offer a more effective approach to navigating the complexities of values in politics and society.

Keywords Politics • Contemporary discourse • Fluidity • Perspectives • Irony • Indifference • Solidarity • Political rhetoric • Adaptable values

"We are a Europe of the values," said German Chancellor Angela Merkel on September 7, 2015, explaining to the gathered representatives of the press that Germany wanted to accept an unlimited number of refugees and that all other European countries must act in solidarity.[1] Values had thus

A. U. Sommer, *Values*,
https://doi.org/10.1007/978-3-031-42159-4_10

once again arrived in the daily business of politics—arrived so definitively that philosophers have begun to talk like politicians. From the self-proclaimed "radical leftist" Slavoj Žižek (b. 1949), for example, comes support for the refugee-welcoming policy of Angela Merkel, but also the concern that "uncoordinated immigration [might] endanger the core of Europe [...] because we Europeans are threatening to abandon what is best and most valuable about Europe," namely the "values" of "universalism, human rights, solidarity, Enlightenment. That, for me, comprises the heart of Europe." "We must stick to these values, when people start coming from other cultures to us."[2] It sounds like a soundbite from some random small-town conservative politician or like the "normative project" of a certain not-quite-so-random court historian to the Social Democratic Party of Germany. That what's at the "heart of Europe" might in fact be *conflict* over values, over highly divergent normative projects, has to be ignored for the sake of a quiet life—as does the fact that for the vast majority of its history "Europe" did not uphold the "values" Žižek proclaims. That even philosophers who without embarrassment credit themselves with making "radical gestures"[3] exhibit such an enthusiasm for confessions of faith might point to an ideological de-ambiguation of the possibilities of thinking and feeling, structurally analog to other fundamentalisms.

But it is by no means the case that "universalism, human rights, solidarity, Enlightenment" are currently managing to stake out a definitive, privileged validity for themselves in today's politics. One month after the government press statement, an image did the rounds of the newspapers showing a recalcitrant citizen holding a large banner reading: "Stop the refugee chaos! / Preserve German culture + values. / DETHRONE MERKEL."[4] The concerned citizen seems to have other values in mind than those of the German chancellor and the "radical leftist" philosopher. Then we have the editor of the Frankfurter Allgemeine Zeitung, Berthold Kohler (b. 1961), who said after the Paris terrorist attacks of November 13, 2015, that what mattered now was "the resolution of the West. And that the West demonstrates its will and its ability to protect its values. In the light of the scale of the threat and the asymmetries of the conflict, this won't be possible without at least some restrictions of the liberties that it is essential to defend, and perhaps not also without sending our own troops to Syria. Without sacrifices, we won't stand the test of this epochal struggle. To prevail in the confrontation with terrorism, one must not allow oneself to be cowed and blackmailed by it. [...] Liberty, equality, and fraternity (as well as solidarity with the world's poor and persecuted) have long-since also become German ideals. But a fourth value belongs alongside them, without which everything else comes to nothing—security."[5] Under the pressure of events, Kohler's dialectical audacity exceeds Žižek's by far: We are to defend our values by restricting our values—sacrifice freedom for the sake of freedom. To make this possible, a new "value" is inserted in front of "liberty, equality, and fraternity," without which these are "nothing"—just as for St. Paul "faith" and "hope" are nothing without "love."[6] But Kohler isn't piously and apostolically thinking of love and of Jesus' commandment "resist not evil";[7] he's referring to "security," in the service of which he deems it fitting to send troops to Syria.[8] In 2004, the then German federal defense minister Peter Struck proclaimed "It's not only in the Hindu Kush that our security is defended, but that's one of the places where it is,"[9] while the CDU parliamentarian Norbert Röttgen today argues "In Syria we are defending our security."[10]

Clearly, there have already been repeated failed attempts to defend our security—a failure that arises from the eminent discrepancy between felt security and objective security. De facto, the security of life and limb in European societies has never been as great as it is today. As dreadful as it is to be a direct or indirect victim of a terrorist attack, the probability of being the victim of a deadly traffic accident remains many times higher. Even this danger is constantly declining: While there were 8162 traffic deaths in France in 2001, by 2014 the figure was only 3384.[11] Nevertheless, it's by no means the case that increasing objective security causes felt security to rise—on the contrary, it seems as if, above a certain level, an inverse relationship develops between objective and felt security. The greater objective security becomes, the more felt security evaporates. We'll only feel truly secure when the last person is behind bars—ourselves included.

Such an unstable security-sense can be pulverized with little effort by anyone with a relevant interest. This extremely effective logic is behind terrorist acts, whether they be committed by Jacobins, secret agents, or IS fighters. In Paris, on November 13, 2015, for example, with minimal means (eight terrorists), an attack on some neuralgic points of the public sphere managed to achieve a maximum death toll and, above all, the demoralization of a whole nation. This type of asymmetrical fight imposes its own agenda on the supposedly freedom-loving Europeans. Interestingly, it's another sense of the "value" of security, a religiously inflated form, an unshakable sureness of one's own convictions, that essentially motivates the violent Islamists: They bomb that which conflicts with their feeling of security. So there's something chilling about seeing an avowed enemy of terrorism prioritizing security over other values.

One of the targets for the suicide-bombers on November 13, 2015 was a café called Comptoir Voltaire. Apart from the perpetrator, whose explosives didn't have the desired effect, there were no victims of this attack.

Aside from the security discourse, what really happens when politicians, philosophers, intellectuals use the V-word? How does V-word communication work in daily political business? What does it do to its recipients? The findings upon which one could base some answers to this are polymorphous. When the chancellor speaks about how "we are a Europe of the values," then the aspiration for togetherness is in first place: Here, "we" are not *Charlie* but values, the "Europe of the values." You could derive from this that those who are neither "we" nor "Europe" have to carve out an existence in some bleak values-desert—especially as values are mentioned here with the definite, rather than the indefinite, article. Not the "Europe of values" but the "Europe of the values." Probably, however, the chancellor's statement wasn't meant in any ostracizing way and wasn't supposed to mean that values, or *the* values, don't exist outside Europe. This utterance was probably based more on a universal, inclusive idea, the cause of placing oneself in an embrace-like relationship with the whole world. Europe offers you that which your heart desires. Knock and the door shall be opened to you. The point is, there's no hint at what these values actually are. Every hearer can picture whatever appeals to them—which will probably be different in a refugee camp near the Syrian border than in a Stuttgart living room.

This is a typical feature of political use of the V-word. The greatest possible non-bindingness and non-determinedness combine with the appearance of the greatest possible determinedness, fixity, and reliability. But then, as the literary scholar Christian Benne (b. 1972) has noted, the "values foundation" inevitably surfaces from the primal slime of day-to-day political rhetoric. "Values foundation" sounds like something you could build on—your choice of palaces or barracks, churches or chancelleries. But instead of everyone with ears to hear listening to the sonorous name of the values foundation, everyone with eyes to see should look more closely. This values foundation turns out to be a strange thing, doesn't it? Is it the foundation on which the values rest, perhaps consisting of particular preferences issued in the coinage of values? Or is it itself a values-amalgamation, joined so solidly that individual values can't be separated from each other undamaged? And what is based on this foundation? Other values? If so, why are they not part of the values foundation? Are they a different thing than the values foundation, if they're just resting on it? If not, then is it societies, states, business interests, or religious communities? In brief: Wherever a politician thinks they're gazing on a foundation, an attentive observer is gazing into nothing more than an abyss.

The appearance of the greatest possible determinedness, fixity, and reliability is a characteristic of political values discourse—and it makes a significant contribution towards presenting certain actions as having "no alternative," a formulation often used by Chancellor Merkel. This is also the case for those who don't imitate the embrace gesture and, like the recalcitrant citizen with the anti-Merkel placard, aim not at a values-inclusiveness for all but at exclusion. There are certain things that such people don't want to rescue. A philosopher like Žižek wants to combine inclusion and exclusion in order to make his intellectual synthetization abilities more attractive for talk shows—while a thinker like Kohler pushes for the enthronement of a new value, security, which he claims is a values-historical necessity. Despite all this determinedness rhetoric, non-bindingness and undeterminedness are, de facto, deciding factors in political values-use, assuming one wants to remain acceptably "in the center of society" as a political actor.

The political values discourse draws its strength from the phantasms of codification and of power of disposal. To base a political claim on values is to act as if one has the power to dispose of them like a market trader does over vegetables or an investment banker over capital. It's also to act as if the *others*—whether they're the political opposition, the immigrants, the xenophobes, the Islamists—don't dispose over values. Values are defended like the walls of a medieval city—regardless of the fact that all walls have long since been razed. No wonder that values are often associated with conservative milieus, where the world is rigid, regional, territorial, and traditional. "Values need God," says a propaganda sheet from Berlin demanding religious teaching in public schools.[12] Or, as the kabarettist Georg Kreisler (1922–2011) crooned: "Shut your mouth and fold your arms, / Christmas is a lovely time."[13]

The political values discourse overlooks just one trivial matter. The trivial matter that values are not static but dynamic—that they make the promise of universal convertibility and mutability. Values don't need a God. Values need history. Values need change.

But perhaps it's a certain shrewdness on the part of politicians that makes them forget this triviality when they extol values in their speeches.

Because how can you speak politically about values if you understand them as media and as products of fluidization? You would have to dream up completely new soundbites, and this is endlessly difficult in the business of politics, which after all largely consists of recycling prefabricated formulas (which is why politics, seen as a conglomeration of specific speech acts, is such an environmentally friendly industry—it gets by with a minimum of intellectual resources).

Nevertheless, political values discourse only obtains its resonance under the spell of change. Values are charmed out and given a distinctive profile by crises. No one sets out to defend values unless values seem threatened. Values become what they are supposed to be only in straitened circumstances—on the left and the right of the political spectrum. What opinion-formers call the "refugee crisis" is an acute values crisis, which in turn represents a symptom of chronic suffering. But this values crisis is nothing exceptional, nothing to justify talk of cultural decline. Rather, crisis is the normal, regular external form of values and values discourse—of both the acute and chronic varieties. Values require crisis, rupture, decision, in order to take form—without them they would remain a word-fog, blown by the winds.

Currently, immigration of large numbers of people from other cultures is demonstrating the non-universality of many local values, values that hitherto seemed invincible as a matter of course. Suddenly they look contingent and relative—contingent on our cultural circumstances, relative to our secularized ways of life. The dominant reaction schema in this situation is values-protectionist: We guard the precious old values with jealous rage and try to shield them from infection by foreign values. This results in cultural parallel universes between which no dialogue takes place, even though we constantly preach that the newcomers must take on our values if they want to live here. If you strip such sermons of their dramatic culture-war stridency, what essentially remains is the demand that new arrivals should attempt to view reality solely with the eyes of those who are already here. They should strive to regard things exclusively from the perspective that people in these parts are used to using. The first mistake here is in denying the diversity of possible perspectives and in refusing to accept the coexistence of multiple perspectives. If the newcomer adopts the local perspective on things, that doesn't necessarily mean that she has to give up her previous perspective. Perspectives can be combined and superimposed on each other. Which is why the second, even more serious error is the lack of readiness to let other perspectives change and expand one's own—the insistence on taking one's own perspective for the only one possible. Every values crisis offers a great opportunity for self-relativization—for relativizing the values one takes as noncontingently valid.

Values depend on perspectives. And because values depend on perspectives, they can't be absolutely valid. Correspondingly, such other perspectives as confront us if we interact with other living beings should serve to expand and recalibrate our own perspectives and thus our own values horizon. That doesn't mean giving up our own values; it means continually readjusting their functionality. Such readjustment is necessary because people, in contrast to trees and stones, are movable beings that constantly have to change their location and take on new perspectives. Every new location demands new perspectives and thus an adjustment of the values horizons.

Being rooted in values is a thought-figure that has been part of the standard repertoire of political values discourse since the philosopher Simone Weil (1909–1943) first described the modern human—and in particular the worker—as tormented by deracination. She contrasted this with a longing of the soul for rootedness, while still admitting that the roots different people need are highly varied.[14] Two hundred years before, when the Enlightenment thinker Julien Offray de La Mettrie (1709–1751) was investigating what it would mean to conceive man as a plant, in order to emphasize the parallels between vegetable and human existence, he did so with the intention of completely disillusioning man's picture of himself and demonstrating the "uniformité de la nature."[15] Weil, by contrast, used the plant analogy to renew the metaphysical dignity of the human, overlooking just one detail in the process: For animal life, including humans, rootlessness is constitutive, because changes of location and of view are defining features of these lifeforms. Again, we are neither trees nor stones. Humans, in contrast to other, habitat-bound animals, are inherently root-defying beings who can repeatedly rip out everything fixed, everything that binds them, and who often enough want to do so. Rootlessness is a defining feature of the *conditio humana*—and that's not a disadvantage but an evolutionary achievement. As mobile beings that incessantly change their perspectives, we need values which, in contrast to the frozen-solid good, final principles, and deep foundations, are flexible and formable.

From this can also be derived the insight with which the literary critic Gustav Seibt (b. 1959) sought to calm the political values preachers in a time dominated by fear of terrorism and migration: "One of the values we are fighting for is values relativism, that is, the admission that we do not know the end-goal of history, and the permission to devote one's own life to one's own values."[16] On the one hand, the European present—whatever else you want to say against it—is a present that probably more than almost any other present grants the individual scope to take themselves out of "operation" without losing face. No one any longer needs to suffer social ostracization if they don't "join in"—almost any lifestyle is accepted (with exceptions for abusing small children), in fact, every lifestyle is supposed to receive recognition and respect. So values seem to be entirely plural. On the other hand, the German present is significantly defined by an empathy commandment, a diktat of compassion, which contradicts the plurality of values and steers them towards uniformity. Many political commentators talk about how hard and cruel the contemporary era is, that we must stand up to this hardness and show solidarity with all the poor and oppressed. Popular culture, films, and novels bombard us with this idea. But why? Clearly, most people don't behave entirely altruistically, in defiance of these appeals. Compassion morality nevertheless gives us a guilty conscience for not acting altruistically. The guilty conscience paralyzes us, so that we simply accept the things as they are and usually refrain from even slightly deviating from the mainstream—from a mainstream that comprises not genuine altruism—not by a long shot—but simply the usual busy routine. So it might be that almost no one seriously wants us to act in the way that the altruism/empathy/solidarity values-catalog instructs us to. It might be that this values-catalog in fact obstructs us from altruistic action by producing guilty consciences, an inner discrepancy, a tornness between *ought* and action. This discrepancy is useful if you merely want to harness people, to have them function. It stops a person from taking their own personal route to deracination—which can be a liberation, including a liberation from the guilty conscience.

Perhaps, politically, we don't need any strictly prescribed compassion and morality. Perhaps a solidarity leavened with irony would be eminently up to the task. Irony means insight into the perspectivity of one's own valuations—the insight that one's own view is by no means the only possible one. Such an ironically leavened solidarity could, in cool means-to-an-end rationality, make more happen than any number of grandiloquent empathy commandments.

This ironically leavened solidarity will also arm itself with a generous portion of indifference. Because in order to do the One, you have to forget a great many things—all the other suffering in the world. To practice ironically leavened solidarity means letting most things simply happen.

Indifference helps to suspend the constant pressure to value, at least at times. To some, the present will come to seem like a great social laboratory in which to learn indifference and combine it with ironically leavened solidarity.

Notes

1. Press statements by Chancellor Merkel and Finance Minister Gabriel on September 7, 2015, http://www.bundesregierung.de/Content/DE/Mitschrift/Pressekonferenzen/2015/09/2015-09-07-merkel-gabriel.html, retrieved on December 15, 2015.
2. Slavoj Žižek im Gespräch mit Karin Janker: "Merkel hat zu lange geblufft". In: Süddeutsche Zeitung, October 20, 2015.
3. Ibid.
4. Mitteldeutsche Zeitung, October 16, 2015, p. 5.
5. Berthold Kohler: Im Weltkrieg. In: Frankfurter Allgemeine Sonntagszeitung, November 15, 2015, http://www.faz.net/aktuell/politik/terror-in-paris/der-kampfgegen-den-terror-kann-auch-fuerdeutschland-noch-folgen-haben-13913127.html?printPagedArticle=true#pageIndex_2, retrieved on November 15, 2015.
6. See 1 Corinthians 13.
7. Matthew 5, 39.
8. "What person will take it upon himself to 'scientifically refute' the ethics of the Sermon on the Mount, for instance the sentence 'resist not evil' or the image of turning the other cheek? And yet it is clear: seen from this world, it is an ethic of undignifiedness that is preached here: one must choose between the religious dignity that brings this ethic and the dignity of man, which preaches something quite different: 'Resist evil, - or you share responsibility for its dominance.' For the individual, according to the last statement, one is the Devil and the other is God, and the individual must decide which one is God and which is the Devil for him." Max Weber: Gesammelte Aufsätze zur Wissenschaftslehre. ed. Johannes Winckelmann. 6th ed. Tübingen 1985, p. 604.
9. Government declaration, Berlin, March 11, 2004, www.bmvg.de, retrieved on December 8, 2015, often incorrectly quoted as: "Germany's freedom is defended in the Hindu Kush."
10. Norbert Röttgen: In Syrien verteidigen wir unsere Sicherheit. In: Frankfurter Allgemeine Zeitung, November 28, 2015, http://www.faz.net/aktuell/politik/kampf-gegenden-terror/warum-deutschlandgegen-den-is-kaempft-13936087.html, retrieved on December 10, 2015.

11. http://de.statista.com/statistik/daten/studie/161034/umfrage/anzahl-der-verkehrstoten-infrankreich/, retrieved on December 15, 2015.
12. http://religionsunterricht-berlin.de/, retrieved on December 16, 2015.
13. http://leisedenker.com/2011/12/19/georg-kreisler-weihnachten-isteine-schone-zeit/, retrieved on December 16, 2015.
14. Simone Weil: L'enracinement. Prélude à déclaration des devoirs envers l'être humain. Paris 1949, p. 61.
15. [Julien Offray de La Mettrie:] L'homme-plante, Potsdam [1748], p. 5.
16. Gustav Seibt: Reaktion auf den Terror. Der nächste Glaubenskrieg. In: Frankfurter Allgemeine Zeitung, November 17, 2015, http://www.sueddeutsche.de/kultur/debatte-um-werteunsere-art-zu-leben-1.2739209, retrieved on November 18, 2015.

CHAPTER 11

Against Prescriptions. Why Values?

Abstract The chapter titled "Against Prescriptions: Why Values?" explores the perplexing question of why humans need and use values, even though values themselves are inherently ambiguous and lacking in concrete existence. The chapter delves into the fluid nature of values, highlighting their adaptability and flexibility to meet the diverse and evolving needs of individuals and societies. Drawing parallels between values and money, the author contends that the emergence of values has been pivotal in shaping modern societies, comparable to the transformative impact of coinage. The chapter explores how values serve as functional equivalents of money, allowing for the comparison and exchange of perspectives and ways of life. It also discusses the democratizing and individualizing effects of values, which challenge traditional hierarchies and domains. Ultimately, the chapter presents values as imaginative and fictive entities that provide meaning and guidance in a world characterized by uncertainty and change, advocating for a thoughtful and nuanced approach to understanding and utilizing values in modern societies.

Keywords Values as fictions • Ambiguity • Moral evolution • Flexibility • Universal barter economy • Values inflation • Relativity • Societal adaptation

A. U. Sommer, *Values*,
https://doi.org/10.1007/978-3-031-42159-4_11

The subheading of this book asks why we need values, even though they don't exist. In German, the question is ambiguous because the word for need, *brauchen*, can also mean "to use." It suggests both that we're dependent on values and that we exploit them. And this ambiguity is intended because, like values themselves, it holds things in balance. It refuses any prescription—and gains yet more power with the undeterminedness of the "we" who need and use values.

So why do we need and use values, even though they don't exist? Because we need and use fictions. Fictions are not rigid but mutable, adaptable to our needs—as mutable as these needs themselves. Values are flexible in their conception, their use, their validity. This makes them more effective than any "precepts," "principles," "duties." Values allow everyone to take their share and to do their bit. We need values because, of themselves, they are nothing, but to us they can be everything (imaginable). Values aren't provided. Values are made. By us, for us.

One day, perhaps, it will turn out that the invention of values one or two hundred years ago was just as decisive as the invention of coinage 2650 years ago. Money equalizes things that are unequal and that don't initially have anything to do with each other; it makes goods exchangeable and services comparable. Values equalize ways of life that are unequal and that don't initially have anything to do with each other; they make perspectives comparable and exchangeable. The decline of the medieval social order of estates was based on the emergence of values. With the arrival of the values, the Ancien Régime came to its end. Values imply that individuals have a choice about how to live, that they can change without being bound to a social role prescribed by their estate. In old Europe, there was only the one good, with different ways of pursuing it depending on the estate to which one belonged. The values perspectivally fractured this single good and tailored it to individual life choices. The values multiply the good.

The path from the money economy to the values economy lasted two and a half millennia. We still haven't recognized the full implications of this journey. Money means a multiplication of the thing-world and of thing-relations. Values mean a multiplication of ways of life that are possible and that can't be reduced to each other.

Today, we are at approximately the same chronological remove from the emergence of values as a guiding medium as Aristotle was from the emergence of the first coinage as a guiding medium in Lydia.[1] Aristotle calmly weighs up the pros and cons of the money economy and abhors the practice of piling up money for money's sake. Our approach to values should be similarly level-headed; we should recognize their advantages in the universal barter economy of life without deifying them. Values, like money, create vast freedoms—but they can also enslave us, if we subject ourselves unconditionally to certain values of others.

Simone Weil objected to money on the grounds it was responsible not only for military conquests but also for the deracination of human beings; wherever it penetrated, it destroyed roots.[2] She condemned money because some have it while others don't. By contrast, we might argue, values are fairly distributed. Everyone can claim them and has free access to them. There's a values surplus. Values also deracinate. But that should be welcomed, not condemned, for the human is a rootless animal that should have the courage of rootlessness. Among its duties is the cutting of the umbilical cord, and here it can draw significant aid from values, which enable it to break with a good that is imposed on it.

Values are functional equivalents of money, in other words, virtuosos of transmission and transfer. They make the unequal equal, or at least comparable and offsettable. In contrast to money, however, values can neither be hoarded nor made artificially scarce; their production isn't the monopoly of central and commercial banks. Values creation and values binding aren't the privilege of particular groups or persons but an option open to all groups and persons. Values inflation enables values creation. With recourse to values, new expanses of territory can constantly be claimed. Values are the expression of a general democratization and individualization. In the dominion of values, there's no longer a "natural" hierarchy of social domains; the long-unquestioned superordination of the religious sphere or of the political sphere falls away. Everything must first prove itself in its value; simple membership of a particular domain is no longer a guarantee.

The value of values lies to a large extent in their capacity, in contrast to the monolithic good, to inflationize and thus neutralize themselves. No value stands alone for long. Counter-values are launched and counter-counter-values against the counter-values. Values give birth to values. "Monumenta fatiscunt ; / mors etiam saxis nominibusque venit,"[3] wrote the late-Roman poet Ausonius (c. 310–393): "Monuments decay, and death comes even to stones and names." Like stones and names, values are not just born. They also die.[4]

Carefully nurtured values, before they die, are a skeptical medium—a medium for neutralizing, for fostering indifference. They take domains that are in themselves separate and render them convertible with each other—for example, the economic domain with the political or the religious with the aesthetic, thus disrupting the manifold claims for validity made by individual domains and their guiding judgments. A complete equivalence between domains is, of course, impossible to achieve—especially since moral values tend to barge their way into all domains and overwrite whatever guiding judgements happen to apply there. Economics, politics, or aesthetics often capitulate before the universal presumption of moral values. Fortunately, moral values are often sufficiently contradictory in themselves or between each other that values neutralization occurs not through domain confrontation but through antagonisms between different moralities. It makes all the difference whether, for example, you make freedom or equality your supreme moral value. The trick is keeping the two contradictory values in a dynamic equilibrium so their antagonism doesn't become destructive but remains productive (as in the democracies based on the Swiss model). Nothing, however, guarantees that such an equilibrium will last forever. One effective rule of thumb for prolonging the equilibrium is: never grant one value sovereignty over all the others!

From a historical viewpoint, values are not merely helpless answers to the nihilism, the supposed vacuum, that the end of moral and metaphysical certainty in the eighteenth and nineteenth centuries created. While values discourse does often sound like stammering, this is more an indicator that it hasn't yet congealed into stereotypical, dogmatic schemata that can be repeated blindly and with the arbitrary repetition of a prayer wheel—at least if you ignore values discourse by politicians. Proper values discourse is uncertain, inarticulate, tentative, because it can't rely on a set of pat formulas—because its filling, like that of the doughnuts Germans eat to celebrate the New Year, is a matter of choice. The usual options are jelly, egg liqueur, and cream, but mustard is also possible. Values discourse isn't some panicky babbling by those who despair that there's no longer a spiritual roof over their heads. To communicate through values rather than through certainties is an act of strength. Thinking in values is a specific modern feat of synthesis, a powerful anti-nihilist endeavor. That each synthesis is highly unstable and has to be constantly rearranged, under the conditions of modernity, under the condition of human mobility, essentially goes without saying. If you take an even longer historical view of the way values have gained the power to shape worldviews, it's surprising how, in the nineteenth and early twentieth centuries, philosophers who claimed to have unearthed values for themselves and for humanity shrank back from their discovery. Whether they were in favor of formalizing values or materializing them, they found the idea that values could be flexible rather than prescribed unbearable. Values were instead supposed to be absolute or at least relatively absolute. The first phase of philosophical values discourse was therefore, with a few exceptions (such as Nietzsche), a phase of values absolutization. When this procedure no longer seemed viable, what with the quicksilver values having resisted all efforts to pour them into some kind of alloy, ethicists ruefully abandoned them, without realizing that it's precisely their mercurial properties that make values of such decisive significance for modern societies. In such societies, a rigid moral regime with only schematic distinctions between good and evil proves just as unviable as a strict, impermeable separation between distinct domains, such as religion, politics, or economics.

Modern societies are domain-erasing and domain-blending societies. And values prove ideally suited as an admixture, an enzyme of culture. After all, enzymes are substances made from macromolecules that catalytically accelerate reactions. Values function as fermenting macromolecules of human sociality.

And when the occasional absoluteness-nostalgist objects that values have become a replacement religion in modernity, the snide undertone is impossible to ignore. The accusation jolts the listener onto the scent that some serious wrongdoing must have happened here. That the true religion has been sacrificed to a fatal values cult. Religion, the argument goes, has been the victim of an illegitimate power grab and values are merely a sordid excuse for hiding this illegitimacy. The fact being sweepingly overlooked here by the absoluteness-nostalgist is that values can, and in fact must, substitute for religion in modernity because, in contrast to traditional religions with their tendency towards inertia and sclerosis, they are highly adaptable and thus highly capable. It could be that the Greek philosopher Critias (c. 460–403 BCE) was right when he theorized that religion only emerged after politics. Gods, he said, had been invented to watch over the actions of humans which, taking place in the shadows, were concealed from earthly guardians of the law. Fear of the gods had, therefore, been dreamt up as a deterrent to the evildoers.[5] Modern evolutionary psychologists such as Ara Norenzayan (b. 1970) sell this idea as their own "surprising and provocative argument," without a single word of acknowledgement for its originator Critias. Great, all-knowing gods were first dreamt up in the Ancient Near East, the story goes, a means of forming the first states in which personal contact within a tribe was no longer enough to govern the moral household. That's why the gods had to come in as invisible surveillance specialists: "Big Gods for Big Groups," because "Watched people are nice people."[6] However you feel about modern science indulging in a Eureka moment here for discovering what's actually been known for 2500 years, you'll take one insight above all from Critias and Norenzayan: That religion is historically contingent, that its emergence and continuance are down to particular social needs. These needs—especially the need to control potentially deviant neighbors—may still pertain in modern societies, but they're satisfied not by gods and the threat of infernal punishment but by hidden cameras and telephone surveillance. Real control has replaced fictive control. *Big Brothers for Big Groups …*

In modern societies, the strictly binary code of good and evil, which may have been enough to regulate pre-modern mono-societies, has been overcome. Values inflation has overthrown the tyranny of good and evil by ceaselessly differentiating, particularizing, and refining. But the usefulness of values is not only that they grant discretion, that their inflation allows everyone their own values. Everyone has access in some way to values, even the pimp or the honor-killer. Values also produce the appearance of a sharedness. We are ceaselessly asked the question (not that it's taken seriously as a question): Do we not all share the same universal human values, regardless of what our worldview is? At any rate, this is what is insinuated when conflict situations occur. This kind of promise that everything can be brought back to a shared basis is essential for the values discourse—regardless of how illusory these promises may appear to the sober observer.

Values as imaginative and fictive entities are appropriate to societies in which the imaginary and fictive have gained a dominant role—in contrast to the societies that were defined by strong religiosity, by the coexistence of an imaginary that was held to be absolutely true alongside the full awareness that what was believed and held to be valuable was imaginary and fictive. Card-carrying values ontologists who believe in the in-itself existence of values are an endangered species, albeit one in which politicians, "opinion-formers," and "media figures" are disproportionately represented. We live in a world of the conscious as-if. Which is why it's normal that the insight into the as-if even of the "normative foundations" applies to values. Values as as-if substances give meaning to modern societies. We need them not because we'd be directionless without them but because they weave communicative nets that can be used to catch the most varied of realities.

"Words, words, words!" shouts a Hamletian objector,[7] pointing out the glaring lack of reality-satisfaction in all these beautiful values. It speaks volumes that the German word for word, *Wort*, is only one letter different from the word for value, *Wert*. Peter Sloterdijk, for example, tried to show "that the 'values' are that which is left over when one leaves out the practice aspect of the virtues—which is why 'values' are the shibboleth of ethics in the age of the discourse, consequently a mere menu ethics whose arbitrariness is surpassed only by the entirely dematerialized discourse ethics, which might just as well be called babble ethics."[8] That "talk" is bad, evil even, is a truism for a section of the bourgeois intelligentsia, committed as they are to a certain dark profundity. But are we on safe ground with this assumption? Doesn't talk keep things moving and compel us to keep adapting our perspectives to the mobility of reality, while the steel-hard virtues simply command us, come what may? It's precisely in their much lower directing force and personal bindingness, as compared with virtues, that the decisive strength of values lies within the evolution of morality. Today, societies in the process of (self-)enlightenment no longer need strictly binary codes of good and evil; nor do they need virtues imposed by authority that demand constant practice and rigid reaction patterns. Virtues stand for coercion, values for freedom, a values politician might say—and I would tend to agree with her, if this didn't sound quite so much like a party convention slogan. True, values are in the first instance just words. But it's precisely there, in the words, that values are made "flesh." Albeit flesh that, like all flesh, is mutable and transient.[9]

Speech-acting has transformed a world in which good, evil, and the virtues rule into a world where it's values that count. This is a powerful moral-evolutionary step, though admittedly one whose meaning is obfuscated by the absoluteness-nostalgists who stridently bemoan the demise of the binary good/evil code or the life-defining virtues. The irreducible diversity of values proves that Western societies have in fact already completed this moral-evolutionary step. Nevertheless, many people in such societies eye this development with the greatest suspicion, what with values being little more than words and thus notoriously vague.

Over the course of modernization, however, not only has the strictly binary code of good and evil been made fluid; so has the no less strictly binary code of being and not-being. Values don't exist like stones and trees exist. In this sense, values "are" not. But they do exist like thoughts or feelings exist. Like the good-evil morality, the being-not-being metaphysics is a relic of old worldviews, no longer appropriate to the contemporary world but still looming into the present. In the vagueness of values is their decisive advantage in the moral battle for survival. Values *are* insofar as they are realized—insofar as human beings lend them reality in thinking, speaking, and acting.

Conceiving the moral-evolutionary step towards values as an opportunity rather than a decadence seems to have become a not insignificant duty of philosophical reflection. Philosophy dislocates perspectives—and perhaps that's all it does, if it does anything at all. Which presupposes that philosophy always proceeds from one point, that it has a location. That it must have this location in order to change it. Like the values, philosophy is a vague thing. As with the values, in its vagueness lies its strength. If philosophy is required to reconcile people with their moral history, it can make use of what the New Testament scholar Gerd Theißen (b. 1943) has called a "minimally invasive moral surgery": Light-touch interventions could demonstrate that life is better in a world of values than in a world of a strictly binary code of good and evil.

On the one hand, values serve toward the constitution of the subject, toward private meaning-making. On the other, they serve toward group constitution, social meaning-making. In doing so, incidentally, values render both the "Big Gods" of antiquity and the "Big Brother" of modernity partially superfluous as surveillance specialists. Because if we assume that others share our values, we don't have to have them monitored by the police. Only quiet doubts remain as to how long the others will share their values with us. After all, values change.

Values don't become accessible in introspection; there's no secret chamber of the soul to which one could descend in order to gaze on values in purity. Values are mediated and negotiated between people—they emerge and transform themselves in the interaction of groups and individuals. And every interactor takes what they please from them. Their choice of values is based not on some insight, protected from all outside influences, into the true nature of the values, but on their more or less independent reception and processing of whatever values-offers happen to be communicatively in vogue. From this material the individual can form, codify, and continuously change their values hierarchies in alignment with their interests—significantly also including the interest in being socially integrated and thus participating in the values of others. We're the ones who attribute values. We attribute values their valueness. Values in this modern sense only emerge with the emergence of self-aware individuals who move more or less freely in the pluriverse of values and are able to relocate themselves at any time. On the one hand, values stabilize groups and individuals. On the other, values dynamize groups and individuals.

Values are always only values for people, for us. And because they're values for us, we defend some of them tooth and claw, while there are others that we casually betray, depending on how things currently stand. Why and how should there be values that are of and for themselves—that apply for everyone under all circumstances? If something so absolute were to exist, it would be—and I'm happy to repeat this once more—inappropriate for such imperfect beings as us. It would be literally not for us. For example, we defend the so-called liberal democratic values (whatever those may actually be), because they're values that we deem to be helpful, fitting, useful, or good. Others may see this differently. But we can expect of those who come to live with us that they make these values into their own—because they want to live with us. That doesn't mean demanding that they give up their long-held perspectives, but it does mean they should partially put themselves into the perspective of their hosts and reconcile their long-held perspectives with this. We can demand this not because we've been somehow granted insight into universal or even absolute values, but because it seems reasonable to us for a peaceful coexistence under the conditions of modernity.

Values aren't mathematical objects that mean the same thing for all (appropriately trained) observers: Values, as fictions, have different forms, different weights, different colors (or in many cases no color) depending on their use, depending on each observer's individual gaze. In some groups, the image we have of particular values is more homogenous than outside these groups. In Germany, for example, the image of the value of freedom is different than in Saudi Arabia. Which doesn't mean that the one image can't or shouldn't influence the other. The German image of freedom will seem attractive to some Saudis, while the Saudi image of freedom, or of unfreedom, may appeal to some Germans.

Values, in contrast to principles, for example, index this insoluble relativity. Values are always values for someone and they're always values in relation to other values. The values' recipe for success is their relativity—which makes life hard for those who continue to talk of universal and absolute values. Strictly speaking, it's a contradiction in terms to ascribe absoluteness and universality to values, because they're always values only in relation to other values, to other things and persons to which or to whom they apply. For modern societies, which aren't exactly wired for truth, values are both characteristic and indispensable. Values don't have to be true in order to take effect, to apply. They're simple. We need values precisely because modern societies, in contrast to earlier societies (specifically Christian ones), have relinquished last truths.

It's the vagueness of values and their boundness in the fabric of other values (which is always an elastic fabric) that comprises their decisive evolutionary advantage in the social war for survival, precisely because their adversaries are unbending truth claims—this is a war, by the way, that's not so much over scarce resources (other than the resource of attention) as over which side gets to impose its interpretation of reality. It's precisely in their plurality, their non-ultimateness, and their historicity that values are socially and individually useful—they thwart the power of all aspirations for unity and absoluteness, and they keep things lively. They blur domains, smash open sealed spaces and systemic enclosures.

To put it another way: We need values because of their undeterminedness and emptiness. Values are screens onto which everyone can project whatever they believe conforms with their needs, interests, preferences. Such projector screens are necessary now and in the future because all kinds of people, with different needs, interests, preferences, must come together in modern societies. They can come together under the projection preamble of values.

Philosophy shouldn't pose as a "values science" à la Heinrich Rickert and Wilhelm Windelband, trying to define the values as precisely as possible (after all, it's usually only other philosophers who are interested in philosophers' definitions anyway). Instead, it should subject values, as imaginary projector screens, to a critical yet benevolent analysis. Philosophizing also means renouncing faith. So philosophers would be ill advised to reinvent themselves as values-believers and values-preachers. But they can conduct thought experiments: What would it be like if there were no values? What would we miss? What would we gain? What help could a group or an individual draw from faith in values, however fictive values might be?

And the philosophers will designate problems. The problem, for example, that the values are arrayed in an imbalanced structure with the moral values in the ascendancy, when the advantage of values discourse lies precisely in negotiability, in the relentless calibrating of values hierarchies. Does the value of values not lie in their flexibility?

And perhaps philosophers, if they offer any advice at all, will advise values asceticism. Perhaps theirs will be a counsel of few values, administered in moderate doses.

Values are fictions. That doesn't mean that they don't exist, but it does perhaps mean that they don't exist without people who create them. Societies, for their part, crave fictions—and the more enlightened societies are, the stronger their need for fiction and fictionalization. Even though, or perhaps precisely because, values are fictions, modern societies are in need of them and can make use of them. If values were physical, natural realities that existed "just like that," they would be as superfluous for human beings as moondust.

Notes

1. On money as a guiding medium see Jochen Hörisch: Kopf oder Zahl. Die Poesie des Geldes. Frankfurt a. M. 1996. Alfred Sohn-Rethel: Das Geld, die bare Münze des Apriori. Berlin 1990 tries to prove that the path-breaking "thinking abstraction" in Greek philosophy can be traced back to the "real abstraction" that was owed to the invention of coinage.
2. Simone Weil: L'enracinement. Prélude à déclaration des devoirs envers l'être humain. Paris 1949, p. 62 f.
3. Decimus Magnus Ausonius: Epitaphia XXXII 9 f. (Ausonius. With an English Translation by Hugh G. Evelyn White. London/New York 1919, vol. 1, p. 158).
4. "Our new Constitution is now established, and has an appearance that promises permanency; but in this world nothing can be said to be certain, except death and taxes." Benjamin Franklin to Jean-Baptiste Leroy, November 13, 1789).
5. Hermann Diels/Walther Kranz (eds.): Die Fragmente der Vorsokratiker. 5th ed. Berlin 1951, Fragment 81 A 25).
6. Ara Norenzayan: Big Gods. How Religion Transformed Cooperation and Conflict. Princeton/Oxford 2013, p. xiii.
7. William Shakespeare: The Tragedy of Hamlet, Prince of Denmark. Act 2, Scene 2, Line 192
8. Peter Sloterdijk: Zeilen und Tage. Notizen 2008–2011. Frankfurt a. M. 2012, p. 517.
9. "Ich bin der Geist der stets verneint! /Und das mit Recht; denn alles was entsteht/ Ist werth daß es zu Grunde geht" ("I am the spirit that always denies! /And with justice, for everything that comes into being/Is worthy of perishing"), says Mephisto famously at the start of his self-description (Johann Wolfgang von Goethe: Faust I. Verse 1338–1340). Because of this, Mephisto has always been accused of a nihilism that wants to cast all that exists into the abyss of non-being. But this is to overlook a crucial point: The emphasis is on the "comes into being". It's not that which exists but that which becomes that is worthy of perishing. Transience is the value of becoming. Is there not a commendable values philosophy in there?

Author Index[1]

[1] Note: Page numbers followed by 'n' refer to notes.

A. U. Sommer, *Values*,
https://doi.org/10.1007/978-3-031-42159-4

Subject Index[1]

[1] Note: Page numbers followed by 'n' refer to notes.

A. U. Sommer, *Values*,
https://doi.org/10.1007/978-3-031-42159-4

Milton Keynes UK
Ingram Content Group UK Ltd.
UKHW020306221223
434809UK00004B/44

9 783031 421587